welcome

You want to crochet, but you've never even held a crochet hook in your hand. You're in good company! Many other crafters are in the same situation and equally excited to give the technique a try.

This quick guide is a great way to familiarize yourself with crochet—its tools, its stitches, and all the basics. Set up in an orderly fashion, *1-2-3 crochet* starts off with topics such as choosing yarns and supplies, then takes you step-by-step through the stitches, and finishes with pages of wonderful projects to make. Maybe you've already skipped to the project section and selected something to crochet. More than likely, your first endeavor will be a set of swatches or possibly a long sampler containing all the stitches. Whatever project you choose to crochet, you'll want to start at the beginning of the issue and master each skill before proceeding to the next.

Of course, it's always helpful—and more fun—if you know someone nearby who crochets. Check with neighbors, friends, and family members to find a crocheter. Or attend classes at a yarn shop or through community education. Your progress will be much faster.

So, find a cozy corner, grab a crochet hook and some yarn—and enjoy! You're ready to learn to crochet!

Have fun!

The Staff

table of **contents**

17

crochet basics

8   choosing yarn

10   setting up your supplies

11   a look at hooks

12   the language of crochet/ abbreviations

13   stitch basics

15   a good foundation

16   crochet in rows and rounds

17   color changes

18   increasing and decreasing stitches

19   keeping tension even and the importance of gauge

20   finishing touches

21   reading project schematics

22   hooked on granny squares

28

34

58

crochet projects

26 hip-hot headbands
Keep little heads warm with these jazzy headbands.

28 cool caps
Everyone loves these super hats—in solid colors or stripes.

30 lacy trim
Dress up a plain T-shirt with this bit-of-lace triangle.

32 granny-square purse
Cute and quick, this tiny bag is perfect for beginners.

34 flower power
Watch your teen blossom wearing these cool fashions.

37 silky scarf
Try this trendy scarf using fluffy yarn and a big hook.

38 triangle shawl
This versatile piece is practical and elegant to wear.

40 suede capelet
The poncho goes retro with this sassy capelet.

42 blast from the past: the granny
The granny is back for a miniskirt, belt, poncho, and cap.

47 hooded sweatshirt
Keep your little one toasty wearing a bright hoodie.

50 super stripes cardigan
Work your tot's favorite colors into this colorful design.

53 diagonal duo
Diagonal stripes make a run for this afghan and pillow.

56 fringed afghan and pillow
Loop accents coordinate this soft pastel set.

58 shearling suede blanket and pillow
For our rugged duo, use ribbon yarn and natural colors.

60 homespun welcome mat
To warm your home, add this cozy rug at the entryway.

62 happy daisy pillow
Give a child one pillow to hug or several for her bed.

getting the
urge to crochet

These days, it seems everyone is crocheting or learning to crochet. What's all the "chain 1, single-crochet 1" buzz about?

PHOTOGRAPHER: KATHRYN GAMBLE

Are you getting caught up in all the crocheting excitement? Drop by your local yarn shop, and you'll truly be smitten!

Even if you haven't yet learned the technique, it's worth a visit to a yarn shop just to be inspired. There, you'll discover shelves stacked with the latest yarns from the world over. Colors from brights to pastels—sometimes combined in a single yarn—will dazzle you. The textures are endless, too: soft, thick-and-thin, crisp, silky-smooth, furlike, and nubby.

And if the yarn isn't enough to get you rallied 'round a crochet hook, check out the patterns. They're spectacular! Today's crochet designers are prolific, providing abundant projects for all skill levels. Look to books and publications like this one for striking hand-crocheted garments and fashion accessories, as well as for accents for your decor.

Never fear—help is here.

When you pay a visit to your local shop, feel free to ask for help—today, tomorrow, and all throughout your crochet adventures. More than likely, the shop owner and the assistants are experienced crocheters. In addition to helping you with your purchases, they should be able to assist you with any reasonable requests you might have regarding a particular crochet project or problem.

Many independent shops—and some large retailers—offer classes on topics ranging from simple basics to granny squares to working with fine threads. You may want to take advantage of one or more of these, too.

So grab your hook and yarn!

Filled with great-looking projects purposely compiled for beginners, this book will serve as a handy reference tool to help you learn and/or refresh your knowledge of the basic stitches and crocheting techniques.

The crochet outlook is bright! Get hooked, and soon you'll fill your days (and spare moments) with beautiful yarns, projects, and soothing comfort as you crochet your stresses away.

crochet basics

Have a hook and a skein of pretty yarn at hand? Then you're ready! This section will help you learn the basics of crochet. It also will serve as a handy reference whenever you need to refresh your knowledge of the craft.

PHOTOGRAPHER: SCOTT LITTLE

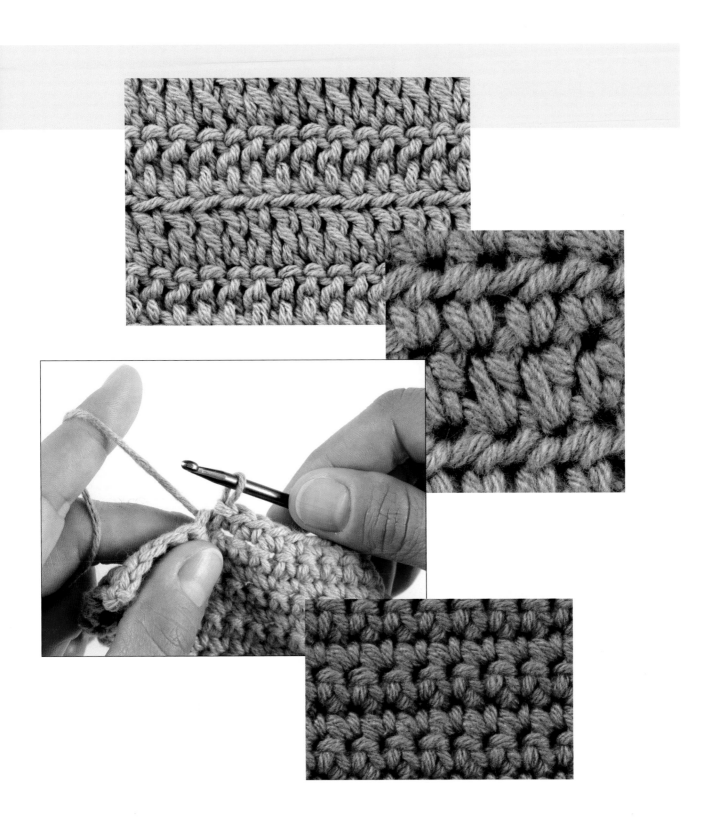

choosing yarn

Selecting the yarn for your project involves more than simply picking out the prettiest color!

PHOTOGRAPHER: DEAN TANNER

You've chosen your pattern and plan to make it just as it appears in the photograph. No problem. But what happens when you get to the yarn store and see all those fabulous yarns? You just might be tempted to make a change! The information that follows will help you become more knowledgeable about yarns and will assist you when making yarn substitutions and selections.

Natural, synthetic, or blend? When choosing a fiber, think about the end use of your project. Natural fibers such as wool, mohair, alpaca, cashmere, cotton, and linen are excellent for adult garments. Synthetics (acrylic, nylon, and blended fibers) are better selections for items such as place mats or children's clothing—the kinds of items that require repeated washings. Novelty yarns and ribbons also

For information on crocheting standards and more, go to www.yarnstandards.com.

are available. If you decide on the yarn before you select your crochet pattern, be sure to ask a salesperson to help you find a design that's appropriate for your yarn and your skill level.

In discussions about yarns, you'll often hear crocheters mention weight. This has nothing to do with ounces or pounds. Weight refers to bulkiness— how thick or thin a yarn strand is. Yarns are classified by weight as super fine, fine, light, medium, bulky, or super bulky. Yarns for baby layettes, for example, usually fall under the fine and light weight categories; yarns for men's sweaters are more likely to fall under medium and bulky weights.

Your yarn selection affects the hook size you'll need to use for your project. Generally speaking, a range of three hook sizes is appropriate for crocheting the yarns in each of the categories. Refer to the chart on the next page for the categories, types of yarn by weight within the categories, and recommended hook sizes.

Yarn labels will identify yarn weight and usually recommend hook sizes. Increasing numbers of companies are identifying their yarns, utilizing a universal system adopted by the Yarn Council of America that makes it easier

yarn weight chart

yarn categories	super fine	fine	light	medium	bulky	super bulky
yarn types	sock, fingering, baby	sport, baby	dk*, light worsted	worsted, afghan, aran	chunky, craft, rug	bulky, roving
gauge for 4 inches in single crochet	21–32 sts	16–20 sts	12–17 sts	11–14 sts	8–11 sts	5–9 sts
recommended hook sizes in millimeter range	2.25–3.5 mm	3.5–4.5 mm	4.5–5.5 mm	5.5–6.5 mm	6.5–9 mm	9 mm & larger
recommended hook sizes in U.S. size range *	B/1 to E/4	E/4 to 7	7 to I/9	I/9 to K/10½	K/10½ to M/13	M/13 & larger

*double-knitting

to choose yarns and patterns that work well together. Look for the weight number on the label that's printed on the universal logo:

On the label you'll also find fiber content, care instructions, gauge and hook size recommendations, the amount (in yards and/or meters), package weight (in ounces and/or grams), dye lot, and color number. Keep the labels until you finish your project. This will make it easier to purchase more of the same—or a suitably similar—color and dye lot should you run short of yarn.

It's a good idea to buy an extra ball of yarn when you're making your initial purchase in case of an unforeseen problem. Be sure to ask about the shop's return policy. Provided the yarn hasn't been unwound and you've saved the label and the receipt, you should be able to return the yarn to the shop for a refund or credit.

Overwhelmed? Don't be. This all will become second nature as you get increasingly comfortable with the craft. Soon you may find the only difficult decision is choosing which project to start first!

yarn weights (shown actual size)

super fine

fine

light

medium

bulky

super bulky

setting up your
supplies

One of the nicest things about crochet is that you don't need a lot of expensive or fancy tools to get started.

The best way to make progress on your crocheting is to take it with you—everywhere you go—in a handy bag. If, like many crocheters, you have several projects going at once, it's a good idea to keep an assortment of bags on hand. They can be anything from plastic sacks to canvas totes to carryalls created especially for crochet.

Also, many crocheters find that if they prepare a small kit filled with basic accessories, they can quickly move it from one project bag to the next. Select a small pouch (a cosmetics one you get free with another purchase is perfect) to hold your supplies. The items at right are helpful tools for almost any project and should easily fit into your kit.

tools of the technique

A Crochet Hook
B Stitch Marker Rings
C Split-Ring Markers
D Blunt-End Yarn Needles
E Thread Cutter Pendant
F Tape Measure
G Stitch-Gauge Tool

A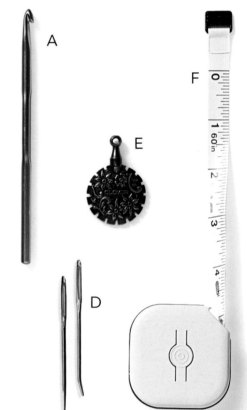

E

B

C

D

F

G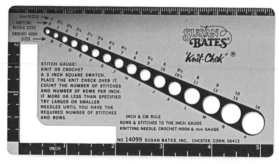

a look at hooks

Choosing the right crochet hook for your project is easy. The project instructions list the recommended hook size; all you need to do is pick out the style or color that works best for you and that you find most appealing.

Crochet hooks are sized to work with different thicknesses of yarn and thread and are easily available in steel, aluminum, and plastic. You'll also find more decorative—but just as functional—examples in hardwoods. Note, however, that wood hooks are not as strong as plastic or metal. So, if you have a tendency to bend your crochet hooks with repeated use, you may want to avoid the wood styles.

The smallest hooks, used with fine threads, are steel. The sizes are designated from 00, 0, and 1 through 14. The larger the number (size 14, for example), the smaller the hook; the smaller the number, the larger the hook.

Aluminum and plastic hooks are larger than steel hooks and are used for working with a variety of yarn weights. They're letter-sized from B (the smallest) through S (the largest).

As you continue crocheting as a pastime, you'll begin to collect more and more hooks. Watch for new designs (ergonomic, for example), and try different styles. You may discover that some hooks work better with certain yarns. You'll also find the ones that are the most comfortable for you to use.

crochet hook conversions— aluminum, plastic, wood

Metric (mm)	U.S. Conversion
2.25	B/1
2.75	C/2
3.25	D/3
3.5	E/4
3.75	F/5
4	G/6
4.5	7
5	H/8
5.5	I/9
6	J/10
6.5	K/10½
8	L/11
9	M or N/13
10	N or P/15
15	P or Q
16	Q
19	S

crochet hook conversions— steel

Metric (mm)	U.S. Conversion
3.5	00
3.25	0
2.75	1
2.25	2
2.1	3
2.0	4
1.9	5
1.8	6
1.65	7
1.5	8
1.4	9
1.3	10
1.1	11
1.0	12
.85	13
.75	14

The crochet hooks at *right* represent a sampling of available styles. Arranged in pairs, the top two hooks are made of wood, followed by pairs of clear acrylic, aluminum, plastic, and steel.

PHOTOGRAPHER: SCOTT LITTLE

the language
of crochet

Crochet instructions, filled with repeated words and numbers, are cumbersome and can be challenging to read. Over time, though, a common language has evolved, providing the crocheter with a kind of shorthand that makes following instructions much easier.

Even so, crochet instructions may seem a little awkward when you begin. Start by familiarizing yourself with the abbreviations listed below and refer to them as you work your projects. *Note: These abbreviations may vary slightly from those used in other crochet publications. A list of standard*

abbreviations from the Craft Yarn Council can be found at **www.yarnstandards.com.**

Once you start crocheting, you'll want to pay attention to the commas and semicolons in the instructions; they set off the individual steps involved in the project.

Symbols are part of the shorthand language, too. Asterisks (*) indicate pattern repeats within a row or round. When there is an asterisk, there also will be a later instruction telling you to go back and repeat the pattern from the asterisk. Work the repeat as many times as indicated. For example, if the pattern

indicates you are to repeat from the asterisk twice more, you'll work those stitches a total of three times.

Sometimes asterisks appear in pairs—a beginning and an ending asterisk—and you'll be instructed to repeat the pattern between the asterisks.

Parentheses ( ) and brackets [ ] also indicate repetition. Repeat the instructions within the parentheses or brackets the total number of times indicated before beginning the next step in the instructions.

abbreviations

approx	approximate(ly)	dec	decrease(s)(ing)	rem	remain(s)(ing)
beg	begin(s)(ning)	est	established	rep	repeat
bet	between	FL	front loop(s)	rev sc	reverse single crochet
BL	back loop(s)	FPdc	front post double crochet	rnd(s)	round(s)
CC	contrasting color	foll	follow(s)(ing)	RS	right side(s)
ch-	refers to a chain or space previously made (for example, ch-1 space)	fp	front post	sc	single crochet
		grp	group(s)	sk	skip
		hdc	half double crochet	sl st	slip stitch
ch(s)	chain(s)	inc	increase	sp	space
cl(s)	cluster(s)	lp(s)	loops	st(s)	stitch(es)
cm	centimeter(s)	MC	main color	tr	treble crochet
cont	continue	m	meter(s)	tog	together
dc	double crochet	mm	millimeter(s)	WS	wrong side(s)
dc2tog	double crochet two stitches together	oz.	ounce(s)	yd(s).	yard(s)
		p	picot	yo	yarn over
		pat	pattern		

stitch basics

Use these illustrations and instructions to learn the basic stitches and to increase your stitch repertoire.

PHOTOGRAPHER: SCOTT LITTLE

slip knot

1. Make a loop; then hook another loop through it.
2. Tighten gently and slide the knot up to the hook.

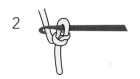

chain stitch (ch)

1. Yarn over hook and draw the yarn through to form a new loop without tightening the previous one.

Repeat to form as many chains as required. Do not count the slip knot as a chain stitch.

slip stitch (sl st)

This is the shortest crochet stitch and unlike other stitches is not used on its own to produce a fabric. It is used for joining and shaping and, when needed, for carrying yarn to another part of the fabric for the next stage.

1. Insert the hook into the work (second chain from hook), yarn over, and draw the yarn through both the work and the loop on the hook in one movement.
2. To join chains into a ring with a slip stitch, insert the hook into the first chain, yarn over, and draw through both the work and the yarn on the hook in one movement.

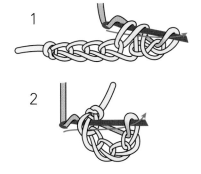

single crochet (sc)

1. Insert the hook into the work (second chain from hook on the starting chain).
2. *Yarn over the hook and draw yarn through the work only.
3. Yarn over the hook again and draw the yarn through both loops on the hook—one single crochet made.

Insert the hook into the next stitch; repeat from * in step 2.

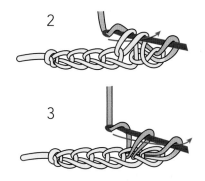

single crochet

fixing errors in your work

Correcting mistakes in crocheted work is easy. Simply remove the hook from the work and pull out the stitches until the error is removed. Establish where you are in your pattern and continue crocheting from that point.

half double crochet (hdc)

1. Yarn over the hook and insert the hook into the work (third chain from the hook on the starting chain).
2. *Yarn over the hook and draw through the work only.
3. Yarn over the hook again and draw through all three loops on the hook—one half double crochet made.

   Yarn over the hook, insert the hook into the next stitch; repeat from * in step 2.

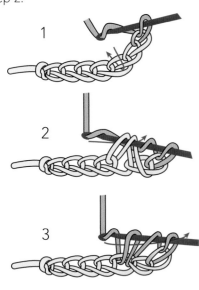

half double crochet

double crochet (dc)

1. Yarn over the hook and insert the hook into the work (fourth chain from the hook on the starting chain).
2. *Yarn over the hook and draw through the work only.
3. Yarn over the hook and draw through the first two loops only.
4. Yarn over the hook and draw through the last two loops on the hook—one double crochet made.

5. Yarn over the hook, insert the hook into the next stitch; repeat from * in step 2.

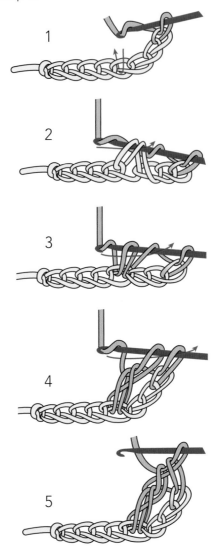

double crochet

treble crochet (tr)

1. Yarn over the hook twice and insert the hook into the work (fifth chain from the hook on the starting chain).
2. Yarn over the hook and draw through the work only—four loops are on the hook.
3. Yarn over the hook and draw through the first two loops on the hook—three loops are on the hook.
4. Yarn over the hook and draw through the next two loops on the hook—two loops remain on the hook.
5. Yarn over the hook again and draw through the remaining two loops on the hook—one treble crochet made.

   Repeat steps 1–5, working a treble crochet in each chain across.

treble crochet

reverse single crochet (rev sc)

This stitch is perfect for finishing the edges of a crochet project. You work this stitch from left to right instead of right to left—that's why it's called reverse (or backward) single crochet.

   Starting on the left side of the crocheted piece with a new color of yarn, pull a loop through the end stitch and chain one.

1. Starting on the left side of the crocheted piece, *push the hook from the front to the back of the (end) stitch and catch the yarn with the hook.
2. Pull the yarn through the work but not through the loop on the hook. Yarn over the hook and pull it through the two loops on the hook—one reverse single crochet made; repeat from * in step 1.

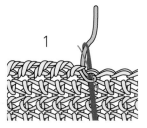

1

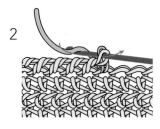

2

working in the back loops (BL) and front loops (FL)

● Back loops: Working stitches in the back loops results in a ridge on the side that faces you.

The pattern directions will indicate when to work in the back loops. (When directions are not specific, always work under the two top loops of the stitches.)

Working in the back loops means you work in the back single strand of the stitch of the previous row. When working in rows, you must tilt your work to locate the strand; when working in rounds, this strand lies along the rim of the outside edge.

● Front loops: The pattern may indicate you are to work in the front loops of the stitches, creating a ridge on the opposite side. In this case, work the stitches in the front strand of the stitch of the previous row.

back loops

front loops

a good foundation

For projects that are well made and pleasing to the eye, always start with a solid foundation.

It is important to begin the first row of a pattern by working the first stitch in the appropriate chain. Although the project instructions will tell you which chain to work in, this information is helpful when learning stitches, making practice swatches, and creating your own straight-edge projects (for example, working rows of single crochet for a table mat or rows of double crochet for a rug).

When starting a row of stitches after completing a foundation chain, work as follows:
● Work the first single crochet in the second chain from the hook.
● Work the first half double crochet in the third chain.
● Work the first double crochet in the fourth chain.
● Work the first treble crochet in the fifth chain from the hook.

Except in rows of single crochet, the group of chains preceding the first stitch counts as the first stitch in the next row.

crochet in rows and rounds

When crocheting, you'll work your project either in rows or rounds. Practice both methods to learn how swatches grow.

PHOTOGRAPHER: SCOTT LITTLE

CROCHET IN ROWS

You've made your foundation chain and worked the first row of stitches. To begin the second row of stitches, you'll need to turn your work over.

Before turning your work over, however, you must work the required number of "turning chains." Turning chains raise the level of your work along the edge to equal the height of the stitches in the next row. Work the required number of chain(s); then, without removing the hook, turn the work over to the opposite side and begin the second (or next) row.

With the exception of single crochet, all turning chains count as the first stitch of the row. Following are guidelines for establishing the number of chains when working a straight-edged piece.

To begin a row of single crochets, chain one, turn, and work the first single crochet in the first stitch of the row. For a row of half double crochets, chain two, turn, and work the first half double in the second stitch of the row. To begin a row of double crochets, chain three, turn, and work the first double in the second stitch of the row. For a row of treble crochets, chain four, turn, and work the first treble in the second stitch of the row.

Also, notice the tiny holes at the tops of the stitches. Insert the hook into these holes so that you are working to the left of each stitch of the previous row. Keep this in mind as you crochet, especially when you work patterns that skip stitches.

Except for single crochet, the last stitch of each row is worked in the top of the turning chain. Always work under two loops of the turning chain to avoid a hole in your work.

CROCHET IN ROUNDS

Unlike patterns crocheted back and forth in rows, motifs such as circles, hexagons, some squares (such as granny squares), and other medallion shapes are stitched in rounds that begin in the center of the shape. When you have stitched completely around the shape, you have completed one round. In most instances, you'll work with the right side facing you.

As you crochet each stitch, insert the hook into the hole to the right of the stitch in the round below (the opposite of when working in rows).

Increases are a part of crocheting in rounds, and instructions cite specifically the number of stitches required to keep the work lying flat. As the motif increases in size, so will the number of stitches in each round. *Note: If your piece does not lie flat, stop and recheck your tension and pattern instructions.*

Most rounds are joined with a slip stitch in the top of the beginning chain of the round. Work this slip stitch under two loops of the chain to avoid a hole in your work.

color changes

The method for making a color change depends on the stitch, whether you're working in rows or rounds, and where the color change occurs.

PHOTOGRAPHER: SCOTT LITTLE

CHANGING COLORS IN ROWS

Within a Row

For a single-crochet (sc) color change: With the yarn color in use, draw up a loop in the stitch before the color change; pull a loop of the new color through both loops on the hook (see the photo *below*); work sc in next stitch with the new color.

For a half-double-crochet (hdc) color change: With the yarn color in use, yarn over, draw up a loop in the stitch before the color change; with the new color, draw through all three loops on hook. Work next hdc with new color.

For a double-crochet (dc) color change: With yarn color in use, draw up a loop in the stitch before the color change, yarn over and draw through two loops; draw a loop of the new color through remaining two loops on hook (see the photo *below*). Work a dc in the next stitch with the new color.

For a treble-crochet (tr) color change: With yarn color in use, yarn over hook twice and draw up a loop in the stitch before the color change, (yarn over and draw through two loops on hook) twice; draw a loop of the new color through the remaining two loops on the hook. Work a tr in next stitch with new color.

At the End of a Row

Complete the number of stitches in a row. With the new color, draw up a loop in the last stitch on the hook, work the required number of chains for the next row, turn the work, and begin the row with the new color.

CHANGING COLORS IN ROUNDS

Cutting off the yarn means that you are going to join another yarn or that you have completed your project. The instructions will tell you where to add the new color. Generally, you'll join the yarn color with a slip stitch.

For granny squares, you may be instructed to draw up a loop in a specified chain-space (see photo *above*).

increasing and decreasing stitches

Once you've mastered the basic crochet stitches, you'll find increasing and decreasing easy to do.

INCREASING STITCHES

Working increases makes your crochet piece wider or fuller.

In most instances, increasing is used to shape garments or to achieve pattern effects. Increases can be worked anyplace in a row or round, although pattern instructions usually specify where they occur. The most common method for increasing is to work two stitches into one stitch in the previous row or round.

When instructions indicate that increases are to be evenly spaced across the row or round, it is best to first calculate the number of stitches between each increase before beginning the next row or round. For example, when you are working on a piece that is 80 stitches across and the directions tell you to increase 10 stitches evenly spaced, divide 10 into 80 to determine that you need to work an increase on every eighth stitch.

DECREASING STITCHES

Decreasing stitches makes your crochet piece narrower.

As with increasing, decreasing is used for garment shaping or pattern effects. The method of decreasing depends on the stitch you're using. Following are instructions for each stitch.

single crochet

Single-crochet two stitches together (sc2tog): Work single crochets to the stitch preceding where the decrease begins, then draw up a loop in each of the next two single crochets. Wrap the yarn over the hook (yarn over) and draw the strand through all three loops on the hook. One stitch is made from working over two.

half double crochet

Half-double-crochet two stitches together (hdc2tog): Work half double crochets to the stitch preceding where the decrease begins. Wrap the yarn over the hook (yarn over) and draw up a loop in each of the next two half double crochets; wrap the yarn over the hook and draw the strand through all four loops on the hook. One stitch is made from working over two.

double crochet

Double-crochet two stitches together (dc2tog): Work double crochets to the stitch preceding the point of decrease. Wrap the yarn over the hook (yarn over) and draw up a loop in the next double crochet; wrap the yarn over the hook and draw the strand through two loops on the hook. Wrap the yarn over the hook and draw up a loop in the next double crochet; wrap the yarn over the hook and draw through two loops on the hook; then wrap the yarn over the hook and draw through the remaining three loops on the hook. One stitch is made from working over two.

treble crochet

Treble-crochet two stitches together (tr2tog): Work treble crochets to the stitch preceding the point of decrease. Wrap the yarn over the hook (yarn over) twice and draw up a loop in the next treble crochet; (wrap the yarn over the hook and draw the strand through two loops on the hook) twice. Wrap the yarn over the hook twice and draw up a loop in the next treble crochet; (wrap the yarn over the hook and draw the strand through the two loops on the hook) twice; wrap yarn over the hook and draw through the remaining three loops on the hook. One stitch is made from working over two.

keeping tension even and the importance of gauge

With practice, you'll become increasingly comfortable with manipulating the hook, and the look of your stitching will improve.

PHOTOGRAPHER: SCOTT LITTLE

KEEPING TENSION EVEN

Once you learn a stitch and get into the rhythm of crocheting it, you'll want to consider your tension.

When the tension of your work (or crochet "fabric") is even, all your stitches will look and lie the same. These suggestions will help you get your tension right.

• For stitches that are even and uniform in size, crochet over the shank, or widest part, of the hook. You'll have better control over your stitches if you keep the thumb and middle finger of your left hand close to the area where you are stitching.

• To avoid stitching too tightly, draw up the loop for the stitch you're making and allow this loop to be almost twice as large as the loop already on the hook. As a result, the finished fabric will be soft and flexible rather than stiff.

• When working with fine crochet thread, it is better to keep the tension tighter than when working with yarn. Continue to work off the shank of the hook, but keep the stitches that are coming off the hook the same size as the crochet hook.

In general, practice with a larger hook and a smooth, light-color yarn so you can see your work easily. As you begin to recognize stitches and perfect your technique, you'll be able to move on to more involved projects.

THE IMPORTANCE OF GAUGE

Whether you're making a garment, an afghan, or a simple place mat, you'll want your project to turn out the size indicated in the instructions. Before you begin a project, work a swatch and make adjustments so you are crocheting to "gauge."

Most crochet patterns include a gauge notation. The gauge, or the number of stitches or rows per inch, normally is determined by the hook rather than the weight of the yarn. For example, if the gauge for your project is 16 stitches and 9 rows = 4" using the recommended hook size, you'll want to crochet a swatch with the suggested yarn (or a suitable substitute). Then, using a ruler or a gauge tool, measure the width of the stitches per inch in the center of the swatch.

If you have too many stitches per inch, you're working too tightly. You'll need to stitch with less tension or change to a larger hook.

If you have too few stitches per inch, you're working too loosely. You'll need to stitch with greater tension or change to a smaller hook.

Note: Gauge notations appear with the instructions for all projects in this publication.

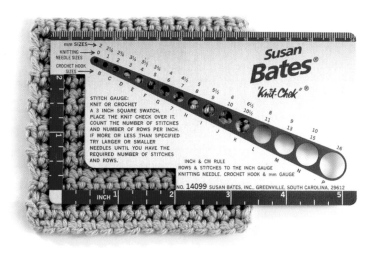

finishing touches

You've worked the last stitch in your project. Now all you have to do is fasten off and finish the yarn tails to make it neat.

PHOTOGRAPHER: SCOTT LITTLE

When instructions tell you to fasten off, in most instances they mean that you have finished your project. *Note: For some designs (for example, a granny square), it also may mean that you are making a color change.*

To fasten off yarn at the end of a project, finish the last round or row, then chain one (yarn over hook, *below*; draw the loop through, *right*). Cut yarn, leaving a 4" or 5" tail. Pull the hook away from the work until the tail goes through the chain-loop. Pull on the tail to tighten the resulting knot.

When you finish your project, you probably will have a yarn tail or two (possibly many more) exposed on the wrong side of your work. To give the back of your work a neat finish, thread the tail through a blunt-end yarn needle, then take the yarn just under the back loop of several stitches. See the photo, *top, far right;* make sure the tail yarn doesn't show through on the right side.

Then take the yarn through several more stitches but in the opposite direction. Clip the excess tail close to the surface.

Some projects require numerous yarn color changes, and concealing all of the tails after the project is completed can be tedious.

One way to avoid having to deal with all the tails at the end of a project is to weave in each tail before you begin the next round of color. Weave the tail into the round you've just completed and finish it off as described at left.

A fast way to get the job done when you're working in rows is to carry the tail along the top edge of your work and crochet over it as you work successive stitches. See the photo, *center right.*

The same applies to concealing yarn tails when you are working in rounds. To conceal the beginning tail at the start of a round, simply catch the tail as you work the first round of stitches in the ring. See the photo, *right.*

reading project
schematics

Use these handy diagrams as guides for crocheting individual garment pieces and for adjusting sizes.

If you've already looked at any garment instructions in this publication, you've probably noticed the scaled illustrations that accompany them. The drawings, labeled with detailed measurements for each garment size, represent the flat, unassembled pieces (see the examples at *right*).

The illustrations aren't necessary for choosing the size of the garment you plan to make. The chest measurement, taken around the chest at the underarm, is the most important factor for that. However, when you need to alter the pattern, such as lengthening the sleeve from wrist to underarm, you'll want to refer to the schematics.

They also can help you visualize the garment pieces' individual shapes (sleeves, front, and back) as you work, and they serve as guides when blocking each piece to your established measurements.

Study the schematics for your pattern before you begin, and then mark any necessary adjustments to create the best fit possible.

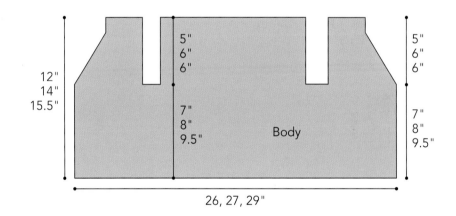

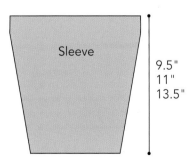

hooked on granny squares

PHOTOGRAPHER: DEAN TANNER

Maybe you haven't tried your hand at crafting these tiny squares yet, but you've probably seen them. "Grannies" have been a crochet staple for generations. Worked in the round, the colorful patchworks make the most of yarn scraps. They're easy to transport, too, and fun for crocheters familiar with the craft as well as those just learning.

Granny squares come in assorted designs, but the one featured here is truly classic. To start, make a slip knot about 4" from the end of the yarn and place it on the hook. Ch 5; join last ch to first ch with a sl st to form a ring.

This action sets up the work for the next round. Keep all stitches uniform in size by crocheting off the roundest part of the hook (about 2" from the tip). When instructions call for working stitches in the ring, work the stitches around the chains that form the ring (insert the hook into the space in the center of the circle). This creates a finished edge in the center. When joining, work at the end of two loops of the stitch to prevent a hole.

Rnd 1: Ch 3; work 2 dc in the ring; (ch 2, make 3 dc in the ring) 3 times; ch 2; join the work with a sl st in the top of the ch-3 at the beg of the rnd. Fasten off, leaving a 4" to 5" tail.

The square of the motif is now established. When you fasten off the yarn at the end of the round, pull the tail through the last loop on the hook and give it a tug to secure it—see page 20. Cutting off the yarn means that you're going to join another yarn color and work the next round with it, or that you've finished the square.

Rnd 2: Join a 2nd yarn color in the 2nd ch-2 sp before the join of the round you've just completed (see arrow on photo for Rnd 1, *below*). **Ch 3, in the same sp work 2 dc, ch 2, and 3 dc—first corner made. (Ch 1, in the next ch-2 sp work 3 dc, ch 2, and 3 dc—corner made)** 3 times; ch 1, join with sl st to top of beg ch-3. Fasten off, leaving a 4" to 5" tail.

You've just completed four corners. Notice that in each corner you've worked chain-two loops between the three double-crochet groups. In each successive round, you'll always work chain-two loops in the corners. Also notice that you'll make chain-one loops between the three double-crochet groups on the four sides of the square.

Rnd 3: Join a 3rd yarn color in the 2nd ch-2 sp before the join of the rnd you just completed and work a first corner (refer to the instructions in Rnd 2); (ch 1, in the next ch-1 sp make 3 dc; ch 1, in the next ch-2 sp make a corner (see Rnd 2, *below*) 3 times; ch 1, work 3 dc in next ch-1 sp; ch 1, join with sl st to the top of the beg ch-3. Fasten off, leaving a yarn tail.

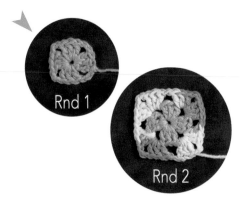
Rnd 1
Rnd 2

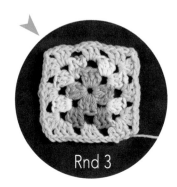
Rnd 3

On this round you began to work stitches in the sides of the square. Those three double crochets are made in chain-one spaces. They will always be made in spaces that have fewer chains than those in corners (chain-twos in this pattern). As you work granny squares, you'll want to conceal the ending tails so you won't have the tedious job of working them in after your project is completed. Here are two ways to do this.
1. Carry the tail along the top edge of your work, and crochet over it as you work successive stitches (see Finishing Touches, page 20).
2. Before you begin to work the next round, weave the tail in the back loops of the stitches in the round you just completed (see Finishing Touches).

Rnd 4: Join a 4th yarn color in the 2nd ch-2 sp before the join of the rnd you just completed and work a first corner; (ch 1, make 3 dc in the next ch-1 sp, ch 1, make 3 dc in next ch-1 sp, ch 1, work corner in next ch-2 sp) 3 times; (ch 1, work 3 dc in next ch-1 sp) 2 times; ch 1, join with sl st to top of the beg ch-3. Fasten off, leaving a yarn tail as before.

When selecting yarn colors for granny squares, you can use every color in the rainbow. Or you can choose a specific color scheme as shown here. Traditionally, grannies are done in a multitude of colors, with the last round of a set of squares worked in the same color, often black. This technique not only frames the colorful squares, but it also makes it easier to join them.

Rnd 5: Join a 5th color as before and work a first corner; [(ch 1, make 3 dc in the next ch-1 sp) 3 times, ch 1, work corner in next ch-2 sp] 3 times; (ch 1, work 3 dc in next ch-1 sp) 3 times; ch 1, join to top of beg ch-3. Fasten off, leaving a yarn tail.

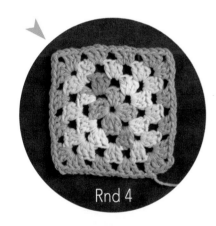

Rnd 4

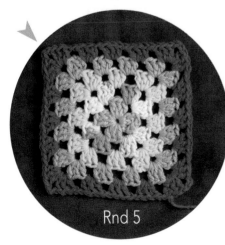

Rnd 5

JOINING GRANNIES
sewing squares together
Use a blunt-end yarn needle to sew the squares together, *top right*. For a flat seam, hold the squares together with the wrong sides facing, then sew overcast stitches through the back loops. Begin at one end in the corner and sew to the next corner stitch by stitch. Sew the units together in rows; then sew the rows together.

crocheting squares together
In the photo, *center right*, the squares are single crocheted together through the back loops of the last rounds. When you crochet squares together with the wrong sides facing, a slight ridge is formed on the right side that further defines the shapes, especially when you use a contrasting color.

joining squares when working the last round
This technique is simpler than it might seem, judging by the complicated instructions that often accompany this joining method. The key is understanding the final round of the square. At times you crochet only one side of a square in progress to a completed square; other times, two or even three sides are crocheted to a completed square. As a general rule, work a slip stitch into the corresponding place of the adjoining square and then work the appropriate stitches in the square that's in progress (see the photo, *bottom right*). **Note:** *In this photo, the last round of the square on the left was worked in lime green (rather than dark blue as normally would be the case) to provide a clearer visual.*

As you work back and forth from one square to the other, you'll get comfortable with the pattern and develop a level of confidence that allows you to do the work without constantly referring to the instructions.

Use overcast stitches to join two squares (wrong sides facing).

Join two squares (wrong sides facing) with a row of single crochet.

Crochet squares together by joining the last round of the square in progress to a finished granny square.

crochetprojects

The best way to learn a new craft is with practice and a **project!**

All kinds of exciting designs for fashion and home decor follow in this collection of 20-plus ideas. Select a favorite to try out your new skills. Then have fun, and don't forget to pass your enthusiasm on!

hip-hot headbands

Need a last-minute present? Crochet one or both of these multicolored bands to keep young heads warm. One design sports a shell pattern and tiny flowers, the other jazzy stripes.

DESIGNER: ANNA MISHKA
PHOTOGRAPHER: ANDY LYONS

FLOWER HEADBAND

skill level
Easy

finished measurements
Approx 3×21½"

yarns
Lion Brand Cotton-Ease (Art. 700); 50% cotton/50% acrylic; 3½ oz. (100 g); 207 yds. (188 m); worsted weight
- 1 ball #102 Bubblegum (MC)
- Small amount #144 Sugarplum (A)
- Small amount #158 Pineapple (B)
- Small amount #148 Popsicle Blue (C)

hook & extras
- Size E/4 (3.5 mm) crochet hook *or size needed to obtain gauge*
- Three small white pom-poms
- Sewing needle and thread
- Blunt-end yarn needle

gauge
3½ shells and 10 rows = 4" (10 cm).
TAKE TIME TO CHECK YOUR GAUGE.

instructions
With MC, ch 14.
Foundation Row: Sc in 2nd ch from hook; (sk next 2 ch, 5 dc in next ch, sk next 2 ch, sc in next ch) twice—2 shells made; turn.
Row 1: Ch 3—counts as dc; 2 dc in first sc, sk next 2 dc, sc in next dc, sk next 2 dc, 5 dc in next sc, sk next 2 dc, sc in next dc, sk next 2 dc, 3 dc in last sc— 2 partials and 1 complete shell made; turn.
Row 2 (RS): Ch 1, sc in first dc; (sk 2 dc, 5 dc in next sc, sk next 2 dc, sc in next dc) twice; turn. Rep Rows 1 and 2 until work measures approx 21½", ending with Row 1. Fasten off.

finishing
Sew first and last rows tog.

FLOWER (make 1 each of A, B, and C)
Ch 3; join with sl st to form ring.
Rnd 1: Ch 1, work 10 sc in ring; join with sl st to first sc.
Rnd 2: Ch 2, dc in same st as last sl st; *in next sc work dc, ch 2, and sl st**, ch 2, dc in next sc; rep from * around, ending last rep at **—5 petals. Fasten off. Place a pom-pom in center of each flower; sew to headband.

STRIPED HEADBAND

skill level
Easy

finished measurement
Circumference = 21"

yarns
Lion Brand Cotton-Ease (Art. 700); 50% cotton/50% acrylic; 3½ oz. (100 g); 207 yds. (188 m); worsted weight
- 1 ball #148 Popsicle Blue (A)
- 1 ball #169 Pistachio (B)

hook & extra
- Size E/4 (3.5 mm) crochet hook *or size needed to obtain gauge*
- Blunt-end yarn needle

gauge
17 sc and 16 rows = 4" (10 cm).
TAKE TIME TO CHECK YOUR GAUGE.

instructions
With A, ch 90; keeping ch untwisted, join with sl st to form ring. **Rnd 1:** Ch 1, sc in same ch as join and in each ch around; join B with sl st in back lp of first sc. **Rnd 2:** With B, ch 1, sc in back lp of each sc around; join A with sl st in back lp of first sc. **Rnd 3:** With A, ch 1, sc in back lp of each sc around; join B with sl st in back lp of first sc. Rep Rnds 2 and 3 until work measures approx 2½" from beg, ending with Rnd 3. With A, sl st through both lps of first sc.
Next Rnd: Ch 1, working from left to right (rev sc), sc in each sc around; join with sl st to first sc. Fasten off. With RS facing, join A with sl st to first rem lp of foundation ch, ch 1, work rev sc in each ch around; join with sl st to first sc; fasten off.

cool caps

Whether you're headed to the skateboard park, the coffeehouse, or the farmer's market, you'll be stylin' in these terrific caps. Single-crocheted in rounds, they go together in a snap using a single color or standout stripes.

DESIGNER: ANNA MISHKA
PHOTOGRAPHER: AKIN GIRAV

skill level
Beginner

finished measurements
Cap circumference = 20"; length = 7"

yarns
Lion Brand Cotton-Ease (Art. 700); 50% cotton/50% acrylic; 3½ oz. (100 g); 207 yds. (188 m); worsted weight

For the striped cap
- 1 ball #113 Cherry Red (A)
- 1 ball #153 Licorice (B)
- 1 ball #158 Pineapple (C)
- 1 ball #109 Blueberry (D)

For the solid cap
- 1 ball #102 Bubblegum

hook & extra
- Size E/4 (3.5 mm) crochet hook *or size needed to obtain gauge*
- Blunt-end yarn needle

gauge
18 sc and 16 rnds = 4" (10 cm).
TAKE TIME TO CHECK YOUR GAUGE.

Notes: Caps are made by working single crochet in the back loop of each single crochet around. Do not join rounds. For the striped cap: Two rounds of each color are alternated for stripes. To change color, work to the last stitch and draw up a loop, with next color complete the single crochet. Leaving a 3" tail, cut and join yarn colors as necessary, working over the tail in the next round.

striped cap
With A, ch 2.
Rnd 1: With A, 6 sc in 2nd ch from hook.
Rnd 2: With A, 2 sc in back lp of each sc around, joining B in last sc—12 sts.
Rnd 3: With B, (2 sc in next sc, sc in next sc) around—18 sts.
Rnd 4: With B, (2 sc in next sc, sc in next 2 sc) around, joining C in last sc—24 sts.
Rnd 5: With C, (2 sc in next sc, sc in next 2 sc) around—32 sts.
Rnd 6: With C, (2 sc in next sc, sc in next 3 sc) around, joining D in last sc—40 sts.
Rnd 7: With D, (2 sc in next sc, sc in next 4 sc) around—48 sts.
Rnd 8: With D, (2 sc in next sc, sc in next 5 sc) around, joining A in last sc—56 sts.
Rnd 9: With A, (2 sc in next sc, sc in next 6 sc) around—64 sts.
Rnd 10: With A, (2 sc in next sc, sc in next 7 sc) around, joining B in last sc—72 sts.
Rnd 11: With B, sc in each sc around.
Rnd 12: With B, (2 sc in next sc, sc in next 8 sc) around, joining C in last sc—80 sts.
Rnd 13: With C, sc in each sc around.
Rnd 14: With C, (2 sc in next sc, sc in next 9 sc) around, joining D in last sc—88 sts.
Rnd 15: With D, sc in each sc around.
Rnd 16: With D, (2 sc in next sc, sc in next 21 sc) around, joining A in last sc—92 sts.
Rnd 17: With A, sc in each sc around.
Rnds 18–25: Cont stripe pat as est, work even on 92 sts. At end of Rnd 25, join with sl st in back lp of first sc.
Rnd 26: With A, ch 1, working from left to right, work reverse sc in back lp of each sc around. Join with sl st in first sc. Fasten off.

solid cap
With Bubblegum, work as for Striped Cap, omitting color changes.

lacy trim

Add a touch of lace to the neckline of a simple round-neck T-shirt. This sweet embellishment takes almost no time to make and adds lots of style!

DESIGNER: STAFF
PHOTOGRAPHER: JASON WILDE

skill level
Easy

finished measurements
Approx 3×3×3"

thread
DMC Cébélia crochet cotton, Size 10
● 1 ball #747 Turquoise

hook & extra
● Size 7 (1.5 mm) steel crochet hook
● Blunt-end yarn needle

pattern stitches
Picot
Ch 5, sl st into top of same dc.

Popcorn (pc)
Work 5 tr in next ch, drop lp from hook, insert hook from front into first tr of 5-tr grp, pick up dropped lp and draw it through lp on hook; ch 1.

instructions
Ch 6, join with sl st to first ch to form ring.
Rnd 1: Ch 6—counts as dc and ch 3; in ring work (dc, ch 3) 11 times; join last ch-3 with sl st into 3rd ch of beg ch-6.
Rnd 2: Sl st into each of next 2 ch of first ch-3 lp, ch 4—counts as tr; work 4 tr into same ch as sl st, drop lp from hook, insert hook from front into first tr, pick up dropped lp and draw it through lp on hook; ch 1—beg pc made; (ch 5, sc in next ch-3 lp, ch 5, pc in center ch of next ch-3 lp) 5 times, ch 5, sc in next ch-3 lp; ch 5, sl st into top of beg pc.
Rnd 3: Ch 4, in top of same pc work 3 tr, ch 5, and 4 tr; ch 3, dc in next sc, picot, ch 3, sc in top of next pc, ch 3, dc in next sc, picot, ch 3; *in top of next pc work 4 tr, ch 5, and 4 tr; ch 3, dc in next sc, picot, ch 3, sc in top of next pc, ch 3, dc in next sc, picot, ch 3; rep from * once more; join with sl st in top of beg ch-4. Fasten off.

granny-square purse

Start with an easy-to-do project that's guaranteed to let you experience the joy of crochet!

DESIGNER: COURTESY OF LILY
PHOTOGRAPHER: DEAN TANNER

skill level
Easy

finished measurements
Approx 7¼" square, excluding handle

yarns
Lily Sugar 'n Cream; 100% cotton; 2½ oz. (70 g); 120 yds. (109 m); worsted weight
- 1 ball #93 Soft Violet
- 1 ball #00223 Violet Veil Ombre*
- 1 ball #01131 Celadon*
- 1 ball #83 Cornflower Blue
- 1 ball #71 Grape*

At the time we went to press, #00223 Violet Veil Ombre, #01131 Celadon, and #71 Grape had been discontinued; substitute other coordinating colors.

hook & extras
- Size G/6 (4 mm) crochet hook *or size needed to obtain gauge*
- Safety pin
- 1"-diameter button
- Fabric for lining

gauge
Granny square = 6" square.
TAKE TIME TO CHECK YOUR GAUGE.

instructions
GRANNY SQUARE (make 2)
Make 2 squares with 5 rnds on each, foll the instructions on pages 22 and 23. Choose varying colors for the first 4 rnds, but use the same yarn color for the 5th rnd of each square. At the end of Rnd 5 of the 2nd square, do not fasten off. Sl st into the next 2 dc and the first ch of the ch-2.

Join squares: Holding the 2 squares tog with WS facing, sc in 2nd ch of both squares (mark this st with a safety pin). Crocheting the 2 squares tog, sc in each st around the 3 sides, working sc in each dc and ch. At the end of the 3rd side, work the last sc in the first ch of the corner.

To reinforce the opened edges of the purse top, work sc in each dc and ch around the sts of the front square. Cont around and work sc in sts along the top edge of the back square. Join last sc to first sc at beg of rnd. Fasten off. Weave in end.

EDGING
Join edging yarn color (we used Cornflower Blue) in marked sc of side edge (remove pin), ch 1, sc in same sc, sc in next sc, *ch 3, sc in side of last sc, inserting hook through the 2 side lps—picot (p) made; sc in next 2 sc; rep from * around 3 sides of square. At end of 3rd side, work 2 sc in last sc. Do not fasten off.

Note: Working into the sides of the single crochets makes the edging ruffle, allowing the purse to look the same on the front and back.

HANDLE
Ch 50, join to sc on opposite side of purse, ch 1, turn. Sc in first ch, ch 3, *sc in side of last sc made, sc in next 2 ch, ch 3, rep from * across handle sts; join to sc at end of handle. Fasten off. Weave in end.

BUTTON LOOP
Join yarn to top of sc just above the first dc of the dc-grp centered on the purse back; ch 12, sl st to sc above the 3rd dc of same dc-grp, ch 1, turn. Sl st in each ch across, join with sl st in same st where previously joined. Sew the button to the purse front. Line the purse.

flower power

For a fashion-conscious teen, decorate jeans and a purse with blossoms. Make a six-petal flower, a daffodil, and leaves, placing a stem wherever you like. For an extra burst of color, add a filet-crochet band to the jeans cuffs.

DESIGNER: STAFF
PHOTOGRAPHERS: MARTY BALDWIN
(PAGE 36), JASON WILDE (PAGE 35)

FILET-CROCHET EDGING

skill level
Easy

finished measurements
Edging = approx 2½" wide
Pat rep = approx 3" long

thread
DMC Cébélia Crochet cotton, Size 10
● 1 ball #743 Yellow

hook & extras
● Size 7 (1.5 mm) steel crochet hook
● Matching sewing thread or nylon thread
● Sewing needle

instructions
Ch 29. **Row 1:** Dc in 8th ch from hook, (ch 2, sk 2 ch, dc in next ch) 6 times; dc in last 3 ch; ch 3, turn (ch-3 counts as first dc of next row).
Row 2: Dc in next 3 dc, (ch 2, dc in next dc) twice, 2 dc in next ch-2 sp, dc in next dc, (ch 2, dc in next dc) 3 times, ch 2, sk 2 ch, dc in next ch; ch 5, turn (ch 5 counts as dc and ch-2 sp).
Row 3: Dc in next dc, ch 2, dc in next dc, 2 dc in ch-2 sp, dc in next dc, ch 2, dc in next dc, ch 2, sk 2 dc, dc in next dc, 2 dc in ch-2 sp, dc in next dc, ch 2, dc in next 4 dc; ch 3, turn. Refer to Filet-Crochet Edging chart, *opposite*, to work remaining rows. Work odd-number rows from right to left and even-number rows from left to right. Rep Rnds 1–10 until edging fits around cuff. Fasten off. Make another edging.

finishing
Block edgings; hand-sew to jeans cuffs.

DAFFODIL FLOWER

skill level
Easy

finished measurement
Flower = approx 1¾" in diameter

thread
DMC Cébélia crochet cotton, Size 10
● 1 ball #743 Yellow
● 1 ball #800 Blue
● 1 ball #210 Lavender

hook & extra
● Size 7 (1.5 mm) steel crochet hook
● Large-eye needle

instructions
Using yellow thread, ch 5; join with sl st to first ch to form ring.
Rnd 1: Ch 1, work 10 sc into ring; join with sl st to first sc.
Rnd 2: Ch 1, sc in each sc; join with sl st to first sc.
Rnd 3: Ch 2—counts as hdc; work 2 hdc in next sc and in each sc around; hdc in same st as beg ch-2; join with sl st in top of beg ch-2. Fasten off.

Filet-Crochet
Edging

KEY
■ = block
□ = space

10
8
6
4
2

9
7
5
3
1

Rnd 4: Join blue thread, *ch 2, working in front lps of each hdc, work 2 dc in each of next 3 hdc, ch 2, sl st into next hdc; rep from * 3 times more; ch 2, work 2 dc in front lp of next 3 hdc, ch 2, sl st into 2nd ch at beg of previous rnd. Fasten off—5 petals made.

Rnd 5: Work behind petals of previous rnd by pushing petals toward the center and working into back lps of each hdc of Rnd 3 as foll: Sl st into first 2 hdc, *ch 4, work 2 dtr in each of next 3 hdc, ch 4, sl st into next hdc; rep from * 3 times more; ch 4, work 2 dtr into next hdc, 2 dtr into 2nd ch of ch-2 at beg of Rnd 3, 2 dtr in next hdc, ch 4 sl st into next hdc. Fasten off.

SIX-PETAL FLOWER

skill level
Easy

finished measurement
Flower = approx 1¾" in diameter

thread
DMC Cébélia crochet cotton, Size 10
• 1 ball each in the colors of your choice

hook & extra
• Size 7 (1.5 mm) steel crochet hook
• Large-eye needle

instructions
Rnd 1: Ch 4; join with sl st in first ch to form ring.

Rnd 2: Ch 2—counts as sc; work 7 sc in ring; join with sl st to top of beg ch-2—8 sc, counting beg ch-2 as sc.

Rnd 3: Ch 2—counts as sc; sc in same st, work 2 sc in each sc around; join with sl st to top of beg ch-2—16 sc.

Rnd 4: Ch 2—counts as sc; sc in same st, sc in next sc, *work 2 sc in next sc, sc in next sc; rep from * around; join with sl st to top of beg ch-2; if you are using 2 colors, fasten off first color—24 sc.

Rnd 5 (flower petals): Join 2nd color in join of previous rnd; (ch 4, sk 3 sc, sc in next sc) 5 times, ch 4, sk 3 sc, sl st in first ch—6 petals.

Rnd 6: Sl st into ch-4 lp, ch 1—counts as sc; in same lp work hdc, dc, 4 trc, dc, hdc, and sc; in each ch-4 lp around work sc, hdc, dc, 4 tr, dc, hdc, and sc; join with sl st to beg sl st. Fasten off.

LEAF AND STEM

skill level
Easy

finished measurements
Leaf = approx 1½" long and 1" wide

thread
DMC Cébélia crochet cotton, Size 10
• 1 ball #524 Sage Green (leaf)
• 1 ball #842 Taupe (stem)

hook & extra
• Size 7 (1.5 mm) steel crochet hook
• Large-eye needle

instructions
LEAF
Ch 11. Sc in 2nd ch from hook, *hdc in next 2 ch, dc in next 4 ch, hdc in next 2 ch, sc in last ch; ch 3**; do not turn. Working along opposite side of ch, sc in first ch, rep from * to **; sc in first sc, sc in next hdc, ch 3, sl st into 3rd ch from hook—picot made; (sc in next 2 sts, work picot) 4 times; in ch-3 lp at point of leaf work sc, ch 4, sl st into 3rd ch from hook, ch 1, and sc; (work picot, sc in next 2 sts) 5 times; sl st in ch-3 lp. Fasten off.

STEM
Make a ch length at least 1" longer than desired length. Sl st in 2nd ch from hook and in each ch to end. Fasten off.

silky
scarf

To make this trendy half-double-crochet scarf, all you need are two balls of fluffy yarn and a size Q crochet hook.

DESIGNER: NANCY WYATT
PHOTOGRAPHER: PERRY STRUSE

skill level
Easy

finished measurements
Approx 9×66"

yarns
Patons Cha Cha; 100% nylon; 1¾ oz. (50 g); 77 yds. (69 m); bulky weight
• 2 balls #02002 Vegas

hook
• Size Q (16 mm) crochet hook *or size needed to obtain gauge*
• Blunt-end yarn needle

gauge
4 hdc and 4 rows = 4" (10 cm).
TAKE TIME TO CHECK YOUR GAUGE.

instructions
Ch 10. **Row 1:** Hdc in 2nd ch from hook and in each ch across row—9 hdc; turn.
Row 2: Ch 1, hdc in first hdc and each hdc across; turn.
Rep Row 2 until work measures approx 66" from beg or until 2 balls have been used. Fasten off. Weave in ends.

triangle shawl

You can wear this elegant, textural shawl in so many ways! Here are two options, and we're sure you'll discover more. This piece takes shape when you start at the bottom center point and increase as you work to the top.

DESIGNER: GAYLE BUNN
PHOTOGRAPHER: PERRY STRUSE

skill level
Beginner

finished measurements
Approx 28" long x 58" wide

yarn
Bernat Boa; 100% polyester; 1¾ oz. (50 g); 71 yds. (64 m); novelty weight
● 7 skeins #81305 Parrot

hook & extra
● Size L/11 (8 mm) crochet hook *or size needed to obtain gauge*
● Blunt-end yarn needle

gauge
3 V-sts and 5.5 rows = 4" (10 cm).
TAKE TIME TO CHECK YOUR GAUGE.

pattern stitch
V-Stitch (V-st)
In same st work dc, ch 1, and dc.

instructions
Beg at bottom point, ch 5.
Row 1: Dc in 5th ch from hook—counts as first V-st; turn.
Row 2: Ch 4—counts as dc and ch-1; dc in first dc, V-st in 3rd ch of turning ch; turn.
Row 3: Ch 4—counts as dc and ch-1; dc in first dc, V-st in sp between 2 V-sts, V-st in 3rd ch of turning ch; turn.

Row 4: Ch 4—counts as dc and ch-1; dc in first dc; (V-st in sp between 2 V-sts) twice, V-st in 3rd ch of turning ch; turn.
Row 5: Ch 4—counts as dc and ch-1; dc in first dc; (V-st in sp between 2 V-sts) 3 times, V-st in 3rd ch of turning ch; turn. Cont in this manner, working 1 more V-st between V-sts every row until there are 45 total V-sts in one row. Fasten off.

suede capelet

Retro goes hip with this fresh update of the poncho. Designed to fall just below your elbows, this capelet features a double-crochet yoke that flairs into a body pattern of easy shell stitches.

DESIGNER: CANDI JENSEN
PHOTOGRAPHER: AKIN GIRAV

skill level
Beginner

finished measurements
Capelet circumference (around the widest portion) = 56"; length = 18"

yarns
Berroco Suede; 100% nylon; 1¾ oz. (50 g); 120 yds. (108 m); worsted weight
● 7 balls #3714 Hopalong Cassidy

hook & extra
● Size I/9 (5.5 mm) crochet hook *or size needed to obtain gauge*
● Blunt-end yarn needle

gauge
13 dc and 8 rnds = 4" (10 cm).
TAKE TIME TO CHECK YOUR GAUGE.

instructions
Beg at neck edge, ch 73.
Foundation Rnd: Sc in 2nd ch from hook and in each ch across; join with sl st to first sc, taking care not to twist sts—72 sc around.
Note: Ch-3 at beg of each rnd counts as first dc.
Rnd 1 (RS): Ch 3, turn; dc in each sc around; join with sl st in 3rd ch of beg ch-3—72 dc.
Rnd 2: Ch 3, turn; dc in next 4 dc; *2 dc in next dc, dc in next 5 dc; rep from * around; end with 2 dc in last dc, join to top of beg ch-3—84 dc.
Rnd 3: Ch 3, turn; dc in next 12 dc; *2 dc in next dc, dc in next 13 dc; rep from * around; end with 2 dc in top of ch-3—90 sts; join.
Rnd 4: Ch 3, turn; dc in next 16 dc; *2 dc in next dc, dc in next 17 dc; rep from * around; end 2 dc in top of ch-3—95 dc; join.
Rnd 5: Ch 3, turn; dc in next 17 dc; *2 dc in next dc, dc in next 18 dc; rep from * around; end 2 dc in top of ch-3—100 dc; join.
Rnd 6: Ch 3, turn; dc in next 11 dc; *in next dc work dc, ch 1, and dc; dc in next 24 dc; rep from * around until 13 sts rem; in next dc work dc, ch 1, and dc; dc in last 12 dc—104 dc; join.
Rnd 7: Ch 3, turn; dc in each dc to first ch-1 sp; *in ch-1 sp work dc, ch 1, and dc; dc in each dc to next ch-1 sp; rep from * around; end with dc in each dc to end of rnd—8 dc added; join.
Rnds 8–12: Rep Rnd 7. At end of Rnd 12—152 dc plus 4 ch-1 sps or 156 sts total; fasten off.

LOWER BODY
With RS facing, join yarn with sl st in any ch-1 sp, ch 3; *counting each ch-1 sp as a st, sk next st; 3 dc in next st—shell made; sk next st, dc in next st; rep from * around; end with sk next st, shell in next st, sk next st; join with sl st in 3rd ch of beg ch-3—39 shells with 39 dc bet; join.
Note: Dc bet shells in next 2 rnds is named "single dc." It is worked as a single st, not part of a shell.
Rnd 1: Turn, ch 3, in same st as join work 2 dc—beg shell made; *dc in center dc of next shell, shell in next single dc; rep from * around; end with dc in center dc of next shell; join.
Rnd 2: Sl st into center dc of beg shell, ch 3; turn; *shell in next single dc, dc in center dc of next shell; rep from * around; end with shell in last single dc; join.
Rep Rnds 1 and 2 until capelet measures approx 18" from beg; fasten off.

blast from the past:
the granny

Granny squares never looked so cool as they do on this miniskirt, hip-hugging belt, poncho, and cap. The granny motifs for each design are actually circular rather than "true" squares, but they're still just as much fun (and easy) to make.

DESIGNER: SVETLANA AVRAKH
PHOTOGRAPHER: PERRY STRUSE

MINISKIRT & BELT

skill level
Easy

finished measurements
Skirt = teen/adult size S; approx 15" long
Belt = approx 3¾×36"

yarns
Skirt & Belt
Patons Grace; 100% cotton; 1¾ oz. (50 g); 136 yds. (122 m); sport weight
● 7 balls #60104 Azure (MC)

Motif 1
● 1 ball #60027 Ginger (A)
● 1 ball #60603 Apricot (B)
● 1 ball #60723 Aqua (C)

Motif 2
● 1 ball #60611 Butter* (A)
● 1 ball #60321 Lilac (B)
● 1 ball #60451 Mango* (C)

As we went to press, #60611 Butter and #60451 Mango had been discontinued; substitute other coordinating colors.

hook & extras
● Size D/3 (3.25 mm) crochet hook *or size needed to obtain gauge*
● Blunt-end yarn needle
● 1" wide elastic, waist measurement + 2"

gauge
21 hdc and 17 rows = 4" (10 cm).
TAKE TIME TO CHECK YOUR GAUGE.

pattern stitches
Single Crochet Two Together (sc2tog)
Draw up lp in each of next 2 sts, yo and draw through all 3 lps on hook.

Beginning Cluster (Beg Cl)
Ch 2, in same sp (yo and draw up a lp, yo and draw through 2 lps on hook) twice, yo and draw through all 3 lps on hook.

Cluster (Cl)
In next ch-1 sp (yo and draw up a lp, yo and draw through 2 lps on hook) 3 times, yo and draw through all 4 lps on hook.

miniskirt
Refer to the Yarns list at left to determine the yarn colors.
Make 5 squares with colors listed for Motif 1, and 5 squares with colors for Motif 2. As you join the motifs, alternate color combinations. Motifs are joined while working the 5th rnd after the First Motif is made.

SKIRT BOTTOM BORDER
First Motif: With A, ch 6; join with sl st to first ch to form ring.
Rnd 1: Ch 4—counts as dc and ch-1; in ring make (dc, ch 1) 11 times; join with sl

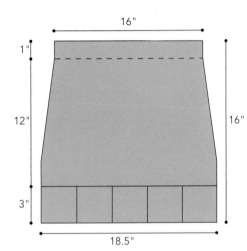

Rnd 5: Sl st into ch-5 sp, ch 3, in same sp work 4 dc, ch 5, and 5 dc; *sc in next ch-5 sp, ch 5, sc in next ch-5 sp; in next ch-5 sp, work 5 dc, ch 5, and 5 dc; rep from * twice more, sc in next ch-5 sp, ch 5, sc in next ch-5 sp; join with sl st to top of beg ch-3; fasten off. Each successive motif will be joined as follows: Work to end of Rnd 4 as for the First Motif.

Rnd 6: Sl st into ch-5 sp, ch 3; in same sp work 4 dc, ch 2, sl st in 3rd ch of corner ch-5 lp of First Motif, ch 2, and work 5 dc in same ch-5 lp of Motif in progress. Sc in next ch-5 sp, ch 2, sl st in 3rd ch of ch-5 lp of First Motif, ch 2, sc in next ch-5 lp; in next ch-5 sp work 5 dc, ch 2, sl st in 3rd ch of corner ch-5 lp of First Motif, ch 2, and work 5 dc in same ch-5 lp of motif in progress. Cont around the motif with no more joinings as follows: * Sc in next ch-5 sp, ch 5, sc in next ch-5 sp; in next ch-5 sp work 5 dc, ch 5 and 5 dc; rep from * once more; sc in next ch-5 sp, ch 5, sc in next ch-5 sp; join with sl st to top of beg ch-3. Fasten off.

BACK UPPER SKIRT
Work across 5 motifs for Back.
Foundation Row: With RS facing, join MC with sl st in corner sp of right motif, ch 2—counts as hdc; hdc in same sp as sl st. *Hdc in next 5 dc, hdc in next sc, 4 hdc in next ch-5 sp, hdc in sc, hdc in next 5 dc; hdc in ch-2 sp; yo and draw up lp in same sp, yo and draw up lp in ch-2 sp of next motif, yo and draw through all 5 lps on hook—joining hdc2tog made; hdc in same st as join; rep from * to end of row, ending with 2 hdc in last ch-5 sp; turn—96 sts.
Next Row: Ch 2—counts as hdc; hdc in each st across; turn. Rep last row, until work from Foundation Row measures approx 3"; end with a WS row.

Dec Row: Ch 2—counts as hdc; hdc2tog, hdc in each st across to last 3 sts, hdc2tog, hdc in last st; turn. Rep Dec Row every 6th row 5 times more—84 sts. Work even until work measures approx 13" from Foundation Row or desired length. Fasten off.

FRONT UPPER SKIRT
Work as for the Back Upper Skirt.

finishing
Sew skirt sides together.
Waistband: Fold last 5 rows to WS and sew in place, leaving a 2" opening. Measure waist and cut elastic 2" more than waist measurement. Use a safety pin at one end to insert elastic through the waistband. Try on to determine fit. Sew the elastic ends together, and then sew the opening closed.

belt
Work as for the Skirt Bottom Border, alternating color combinations when joining motifs tog.

finishing
Row 1: With RS facing, join MC with sl st to to corner sp of right motif, ch 1, 3 sc in same sp. *Sc in 5 dc, sc in next sc, 4 sc in ch-5 sp, hdc in next sc, sc in next 5 dc; in next ch-2 sp work 2 sc, draw up lp in same sp, draw up lp in sp of next motif, yo and draw through 3 lps on hook—joining sc2tog made; rep from * across; end with 3 sc in last corner. Do not turn.
Row 2: Working from left to right (reverse single crochet), work sc in each sc across top of Belt. Fasten off.
Rep last 2 rows on opposite side of belt.

st to 3rd ch of beg ch-4. Fasten off—12 dc and ch-1 lps around.
Rnd 2: Join B in any ch-1 sp and work Beg Cl; *ch 2, Cl in next ch-1 sp; rep from * around; end ch 2; join with sl st to top of Beg Cl. Fasten off B.
Rnd 3: Join C in any ch-2 sp, ch 3—counts as dc; work 2 dc in same sp. *Ch 3, sc in next ch-2 sp, ch 3, 3 dc in next ch-2 sp; rep from * to last ch-2 sp, ch 3, sc in last ch-2 sp, ch 3; join with sl st to top of beg ch-3. Fasten off—12 ch-3 lps around.
Rnd 4: Join MC with sl st in any ch-3 sp, ch 1, sc in same sp. *Ch 5, sc in next ch-3 sp; rep from * around; end ch 5; join with sl st to first sc—12 ch-5 lps.

BELT TIES
With RS facing, join
MC with sl st to right corner of short
side of Belt. Ch 1, 2 sc in same sp, (sc in
each of next 2 sc, ch 80, sl st in 2nd ch
from hook and each ch to end of ch) 7
times; end by working 2 sc in corner.
Fasten off. Rep on opposite end of belt.

PONCHO & CAP

skill level
Easy

sizes
Child 4–6 yrs. (Average Adult)
Shown in Adult Size. Size is determined
by the number of motifs in the poncho.

finished measurements
Child Poncho = 29" across widest
  diagonal portion or 58" around
Adult Poncho = 35" across widest
  diagonal portion or 70" around
Cap = 20" circumference

yarns
Lily Elite Cotton; 100% cotton; 3½ oz.
(100 g); 184 yds. (166 m); worsted weight
● 3 (4) balls #5135 Navy (MC)

Motif 1
● 1 ball #5620 Yellow (A)
● 1 ball #5715 Peach (B)
● 1 ball #5742 Aqua (C)

Motif 2
● 1 ball #5230 Spearmint (A)
● 1 ball #5728 Fuchsia (B)
● 1 ball #5322 Violet (C)

hook & extra
● Size 7 (4.5 mm) crochet hook *or size
  needed to obtain gauge*
● Blunt-end yarn needle

gauge
One motif = 4" (10 cm) square.
TAKE TIME TO CHECK YOUR GAUGE.

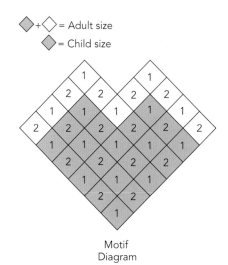

◇+◇ = Adult size

◇ = Child size

Motif
Diagram

pattern stitches

Single Crochet Two Together (sc2tog)
Draw up lp in each of next 2 sts, yo and draw through all 3 lps on hook.

Single Crochet Three Together (sc3tog)
Draw up lp in each of next 3 sc, yo and draw through all 4 lps on hook.

Double Crochet Three Together (dc3tog)
(Yo and draw up a lp in next st, yo and draw through 2 lps on hook) 3 times, yo and draw through all 4 lps on hook.

Beginning Cluster (Beg Cl)
Ch 2, in same sp (yo and draw up a lp, yo and draw through 2 lps on hook) twice, yo and draw through all 3 lps on hook.

Cluster (Cl)
In next ch-1 sp (yo and draw up a lp, yo and draw through 2 lps on hook) 3 times, yo and draw through all 4 lps on hook.

motif

**With A, ch 4.
Rnd 1: Dc in 4th ch from hook, ch 1; (dc in ring, ch 1) 10 times; join with sl st to 3rd ch of beg ch-4—12 dc. Fasten off.
Rnd 2: Join B with sl st in any ch-1 sp and work a Beg Cl; *ch 2, Cl in next ch-1 sp; rep from * around; end with ch 2, join with sl st to top of Beg Cl. Fasten off.
Rnd 3: Join C in any ch-2 sp, ch 3— counts as dc; work 2 dc in same sp. *Ch 2, sc in next ch-2 sp, ch 2, 3 dc in next ch-2 sp; rep from * around, ending with ch 2, sc in last ch-2 sp, ch 2; join to top of beg ch-3. Fasten off.
Rnd 4: Join MC in any ch-2 sp, ch 1, sc in same sp as last sl st. *Ch 4, sc in next ch-2 sp; rep from * around, ending with ch 4; join with sl st to first sc.**
Rnd 5: Sl st in next ch-4 sp, ch 3— counts as dc; in same sp work 9 dc; *sc in next ch-4 sp, ch 3, sc in next ch-4 sp; in next ch-4 sp, work 10 dc; rep from * twice more, sc in next ch-4 sp, ch 3, sc in next ch-4 sp; join with sl st to top of beg ch-3. Fasten off.

poncho

Child: Make 22 of Motif 1; 20 of Motif 2.
Adult: Make 32 of Motif 1; 32 of Motif 2.

finishing

Sew motifs tog, sewing under both lps of sts along outside edge of motifs. Follow the Motif Diagram, *page 45*, for arrangement. Sew motifs tog to make front and back pieces, then sew these sections tog at shoulders.
Neck Edging: With RS facing, join MC with sl st to top of right shoulder seam, ch 1, sc evenly around neck edge, working sc3tog in corners at Vs; join with sl st to first sc. Fasten off.
Rnd 2: With RS facing, join C with sl st in joining, ch 3—counts as dc; dc in each sc around, working dc3tog at corners; join with sl st to top of beg ch-3. Fasten off.
Rnd 3: Join MC with sl st in joining, sc in each st around, working sc3tog in corners; join with sl st to first sc. Fasten off.
Lower Edging: With RS of work facing, join MC with sl st to lower edge of right shoulder seam, ch 1, sc evenly around lower edge, working 3 sc in corners. Fasten off.
Fringe: Cut lengths of MC and Motif colors measuring 8" long. Holding 3 strands of MC and 1 strand of each of 3 alternating colors tog, knot into fringe around lower edge of Poncho.

TIE FOR ADULT PONCHO
With MC, make a ch, measuring approx 1½ yds. Sl st in 2nd ch from hook and in each ch across. Fasten off. Beg at one side of center front on Rnd 2, weave Tie over and then under 3 dc all around neck. Pull up to tighten neck and tie.

cap
Make 2 each of Motif 1 and Motif 2. Alternating Motifs, sew together to form a tube.

TOP OF CAP
With RS facing, join MC with sl st at any corner of Motif, ch 1. (Work 14 sc across top of motif, sc2tog over current and next motif) 4 times; join with sl st to first sc—60 sc.
Next Rnd: Ch 1, sc2tog over first 2 sc; *sc in each of next 8 sc, sc2tog over next 2 sc; rep from * around, ending with sc in each of last 8 sc; join with sl st to first sc—54 sts.
Next Rnd: Ch 1, sc2tog over first 2 sts; *sc in each of next 7 sc, sc2tog over next 2 sts; rep from * around, ending with sc in each of last 7 sts; join with sl st to first st—48 sts.
Next Rnd: Ch 1, sc2tog over first 2 sts; *sc in each of next 6 sc, sc2tog over next 2 sts; rep from * around, ending with sc in each of last 6 sts; join with sl st to first st—42 sts.
Cont to dec 6 sts on following rnds until 6 sts rem.
Fasten off, leaving a long tail. Thread yarn onto needle and through rem 6 sts; tighten up to close opening.

BOTTOM EDGE
Work from *** to *** as for top of Cap.
Next Rnd: Ch 1, sc in first 3 sc; *ch 2, sl st in top of last sc—picot made; sc in next 3 sc; rep from * around, ending with picot over last sc; join with sl st to first sc. Fasten off.

hooded sweatshirt

Complete with a red kangaroo pocket to warm cold little hands, this raglan-sleeve hoodie is just the cover-up for a crisp day.

DESIGNER: ANNA MISHKA   PHOTOGRAPHER: DEAN TANNER

skill level
Beginner

sizes
4 (6, 8, 10, 12)
Shown in Size 6.
When only one number is given, it applies to all sizes.
Note: For ease in working, circle all numbers pertaining to the size you're making.

finished measurements
Chest = 26 (29½, 32½, 34½, 38)"
Length = 14 (16, 17½, 19½, 22½)"

yarns
Lion Brand Cotton-Ease (Art. 700);
50% cotton/50% acrylic; 3½ oz. (100 g);
207 yds. (188 m); worsted weight
● 3 (3, 4, 5, 5) balls #107 Candy Blue (MC)
● 1 ball #158 Pineapple (A)
● 1 ball #113 Cherry Red (B)

hook & extra
- Size I/9 (5.5 mm) crochet hook *or size needed to obtain gauge*
- Blunt-end yarn needle

gauge
15 sts and 15 rows = 4" (10 cm).
TAKE TIME TO CHECK YOUR GAUGE.

special pattern stitch
Seed St (worked over an odd number of sts)
Row 1: Ch 1, sc in first sc; *sc in next ch-1 sp, ch 1; rep from * across; end with sc in last ch-1 sp, sc in last sc; turn.
Row 2 (RS): Ch 1, sc in first sc; *ch 1, sc in ch-1 sp; rep from * across; end with sc in last ch-1 sp, ch 1, sk sc, sc in last sc; turn.
Rep Rows 1 and 2 for Seed St pat.

instruction
BACK
**With MC, ch 50 (56, 62, 66, 72).
Foundation Row (RS): Sc in 2nd ch from hook; *ch 1, sk ch, sc in next ch; rep from * across—49 (55, 61, 65, 71) sts; turn. Work in Seed St until work from beg measures approx 8½ (10, 11, 12, 14½)" or desired length, ending with Row 1.**
Raglan Shaping: Sl st in first 2 sc and next ch-1 sp; in next sc work sl st, ch 1, and sc, sc in next ch-1 sp, work in pat across, leaving last 3 sts unworked—43 (49, 55, 59, 65) sts; turn. Work 1 row even.
Next Row: Ch 1, draw up a lp in each of first 2 sts, yo and draw through all 3 lps on hook—sc2tog made; work in pat across to last 2 sts, sc2tog; turn. Rep last 2 rows 6 (6, 6, 8, 8) times more—29 (35, 41, 41, 47) sts. Work 1 row even.
Next Row: Ch 1, sc2tog, pat to last 2 sts, sc2tog; turn.
Rep last row 3 (5, 7, 7, 9) times more—21 (23, 25, 25, 27) sts rem; fasten off.
Lower Edge: ***With RS of work facing, join A with sl st in first sc at lower right edge. Ch 1, sc in first sc; *ch 1, sk ch-1 sp, sc in next sc; rep from * across; turn.

Work Rows 1 and 2 of Seed St pat, then rep Row 1 again; fasten off. Fold lower edge rows to WS and sew in place, leaving sides open for drawstring.***

FRONT
Work from ** to ** as for Back.
Raglan Shaping and Front Opening— First Side: Sl st in first 2 sc and next ch-1 sp; in next sc work sl st, ch 1, and sc; work in pat across 20 (23, 26, 28, 31) sts; turn, leaving rem sts unworked. Work 1 row even.
Next Row (RS): Ch 1, sc2tog, pat to end of row; turn. Rep last 2 rows 3 (5, 5, 7, 7) times more—17 (18, 21, 21, 24) sts.
Shape neck—Next Row (RS): Ch 1, sc2tog, pat across 11 (12, 14, 14, 17) sts (neck edge); turn, leaving rem sts unworked; turn.
Next Row (WS): Ch 1, sc2tog, pat to end of row; turn.
Next Row: Ch 1, sc2tog, pat to last 2 sts, sc2tog; turn.
SIZE 4 ONLY: Rep last 2 rows once more—6 sts.
Next Row (WS): Work even in pat. Dec 1 st at raglan edge only 4 times—2 sts.

Next Row: Ch 1, sc2tog; fasten off.
SIZES 6, 8, 10, and 12 ONLY: Rep last row (3, 3, 3, 4) times—4 (6, 6, 7) sts. Dec 1 st at raglan edge only (2, 4, 4, 5) times—2 sts.
Next Row: Ch 1, sc2tog; fasten off.
Raglan Shaping and Front Opening— Second Side: With RS facing, sk next st, join MC with sl st in next st; ch 1, sc in same st as join; work in pat across and leave last 3 sts unworked—21 (24, 27, 29, 32) sts; turn. Work 1 row even.
Next Row (RS): Work in pat across to last 2 sts, sc2tog; turn.
Rep last 2 rows 3 (5, 5, 7, 7) times more—17 (18, 21, 21, 24) sts.
Shape neck—Next Row (WS): Work in pat across, leaving last 4 (4, 5, 5, 5) sts unworked—12 (13, 15, 15, 18) sts; turn.
Next Row: Ch 1, sc2tog, pat to last 2 sts, sc2tog; turn.
Next Row: Pat to last 2 sts, sc2tog; turn.
SIZE 4 ONLY: Rep last 2 rows once more—6 sts. Dec 1 st at raglan edge only 4 times—2 sts.
Next Row: Ch 1, sc2tog. Fasten off.
SIZES 6, 8, 10, and 12 ONLY: Rep last row (3, 3, 3, 4) times—(4, 6, 6, 7) sts.

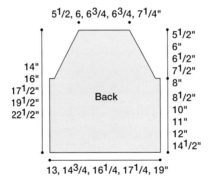

5½, 6, 6¾, 6¾, 7¼"

5½"
6"
6½"
7½"
8"
8½"
10"
11"
12"
14½"

14"
16"
17½"
19½"
22½"

Back

13, 14¾, 16¼, 17¼, 19"

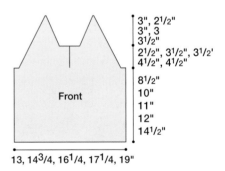

3", 2½"
3", 3
3½"
2½", 3½", 3½'
4½", 4½"

8½"
10"
11"
12"
14½"

Front

13, 14¾, 16¼, 17¼, 19"

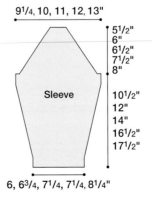

9¼, 10, 11, 12, 13"

5½"
6"
6½"
7½"
8"

10½"
12"
14"
16½"
17½"

Sleeve

6, 6¾, 7¼, 7¼, 8¼"

Dec 1 st at raglan edge only (2, 4, 4, 5) times—2 sts.
Next Row: Ch 1, sc2tog. Fasten off.
Lower Edge: Rep from *** to *** as for Back.

SLEEVE (make 2)
Ch 24 (26, 28, 28, 32).
Rep Foundation Row as for Back—23 (25, 27, 27, 31) sts.
Work 3 Seed St rows.
Increase Row (RS): Ch 1, 2 sc in first st, pat to last st, 2 sc in last st; turn. Work 5 rows even in pat. Rep last 6 rows 5 (5, 6, 8, 8) times more, working increased sts into pat—35 (37, 41, 45, 49) sts. Work even in pat until work from beg measures approx 10½ (12, 14, 16½, 17½)", ending with Row 1.
Raglan Shaping: Sl st in first 3 sts; in next st work sl st, ch 1, and sc; work in pat across leaving last 3 sts unworked—29 (31, 35, 39, 43) sts; turn. Work 1 row even.
Next Row (RS): Ch 1, sc2tog, pat to last 2 sts, sc2tog; turn. Rep last 2 rows 6 (7, 7, 10, 10) times more—15 (15, 19, 17, 21) sts. Work 1 row even.
Next Row (RS): Ch 1, sc2tog, pat to last 2 sts, sc2tog; turn. Rep last row 3 (3, 5, 3, 5) times more—7 (7, 7, 9, 9) sts. Fasten off.
Lower Edging: With RS facing, join A with sl st in first sc at lower right edge. Ch 1, sc in first sc; *ch 1, sk ch-1 sp, sc in next sc; rep from * across; fasten off.

POCKET
With B, ch 24 (26, 28, 30, 32).
Rep Foundation Row as for Back—23 (25, 27, 29, 31) sts. Work 7 rows of Seed St pat.
Shape side—Row 1(RS): Ch 1, sc2tog, pat to last 2 sts, sc2tog over last 2 sts; turn. Work 3 rows even. Rep last 4 rows 2 (3, 3, 4, 4) times more—17 (17, 19, 19, 21) sts. Work even in pat until Pocket from beg measures approx 6½ (7½, 7½, 8, 8½)", ending with Row 1; fasten off.

Edging: With RS facing, join A with sl st at lower right corner, ch 1, sc in same st as join; work (ch 1, sc) pat around pocket; join with sl st to first sc; fasten off. Center pocket onto Front and sew in position.

HOOD
Beg at the edge that goes around the face, with A, ch 80 (84, 92, 94, 102). Rep Foundation Row as for Back—79 (83, 91, 93, 101) sts; work 3 rows of Seed St; fasten off. With RS facing, join MC with sl st in first sc; ch 1, sc in same sc; work in pat across. Work 9 (9, 9, 11, 11) rows more of Seed St pat.
Next Row (RS): Ch 1, sc2tog, pat to last 2 sts, sc2tog over last 2 sts; turn. Work 1 row even. Rep last 2 rows 7 (7, 7, 8, 9) times more—63 (67, 75, 75, 81) sts. Work even in pat until hood measures approx 7½ (7½, 8, 8, 8½)", ending with Row 1. Fasten off.

finishing
Sew Sleeves to Front and Back. Fold the hood in half lengthwise and sew MC edges tog to form back seam. Matching back seam of hood to center of back neck edge, pin hood to neck opening, leaving first 6 rows of hood free for casing. Fold first 3 rows of color A to WS to make casing for drawstring and sew in position. With RS facing, join A with sl st along side of color A casing; work (sc, ch 1) evenly around neck opening, ending sl st in side of color A casing; fasten off. Sew side and sleeve seams.

DRAWSTRINGS
For Hood: Cut 6 strands of A, each 45" long. Holding the 6 strands tog in a bundle, tie a loose overhand knot approx 1" from each end. Secure 1 end of the bundle so it's stationary; twist the strands tog until they begin to kink. Fold them in half and allow the halves to twist back on each other. Knot the end of the cord so that the twisted portion is approx 30" long. Cut the cord, leaving at least 1½" on each to untwist to form the tassels. Trim the ends even. Thread the cord through the hood casing.
For Lower Edge: Cut 6 strands of A, each 60" long. Make cord in same way as for hood, making a cord to measure approx 45" long. Thread the cord through the casing along the lower edge of the sweater.

super stripes cardigan

You can make this half-double crochet cardigan in a solid color, but go for the bold and make it in colorful stripes. Ask the kids to help out by choosing their favorite colors.

DESIGNER: GAYLE BUNN
PHOTOGRAPHER: DEAN TANNER

skill level
Easy

sizes
2 (4, 6)
Shown in Size 4. When only one number is given, it applies to all sizes.
Note: For ease in working the cardigan, circle all numbers pertaining to the size you're making.

finished measurements
Underarm = 26 (27, 29)"
Length = 12 (14, 15½)"

yarns
Bernat Satin; 100% acrylic; 3.5 oz. (100 g); 163 yds. (147 m); worsted weight
All sizes
- 1 skein #4742 Lagoon (MC)
- 1 skein #4712 Palm (A)
- 1 skein #4605 Sunset (B)
- 1 skein #4423 Flamingo (C)
- 1 skein #4610 Sunrise (D)

hook & extras
- Size 7 (4.5 mm) crochet hook *or size needed to obtain gauge*
- Blunt-end yarn needle
- Five ½"-diameter buttons

gauge
16 sts and 11 rows = 4" (10 cm).
TAKE TIME TO CHECK YOUR GAUGE.

Notes: Body is worked in one piece to the armholes. To change yarn color at end of hdc row: With color in use, yo and draw up a lp, draw new yarn color through all lps on hook.

pattern stitch
Hdc2tog: (Yo and draw up a lp in next st) 2 times, yo and draw through all 5 lps on hook.

instruction
LOWER BODY
Beg at lower edge with A, ch 104 (108, 116).
Row 1 (RS): Hdc in 3rd ch from hook, hdc in each ch across; turn—102 (106, 114) sts.
Row 2: With B, ch 2—counts as hdc; hdc in next st; *ch 1, sk next st, hdc in next st; rep from * across; turn.
Note: Ch-2 at beg of rows counts as hdc throughout pat.
Row 3: With B, ch 2; *2 hdc in next ch-1 sp; rep from * across, ending with hdc in last st; turn.
Rows 4 and 5: With C, rep Rows 2 and 3.
Rows 6 and 7: With D, rep Rows 2 and 3.
Rows 8 and 9: With MC, rep Rows 2 and 3.
Rows 10 and 11: With A, rep Rows 2 and 3.
Rep Rows 2–11 for Stripe Pat.
Work even in Stripe Pat until piece measures approx 7 (8, 9½)" from beg, ending with a WS row.

RIGHT FRONT

Working in Stripe Pat as est, proceed as follows:

Row 1 (RS): Ch 2, work Pat across first 21 (23, 25) sts; turn, leaving rem sts unworked. Cont on Right Front only, work 1 row even in Pat.

Shape neck—Next Row (RS): Ch 2, hdc in first st, hdc2tog over next 2 sts, work Pat to end of row; turn.

Next Row: Ch 2, work Pat to last 3 sts, hdc2tog over next 2 sts, hdc in last st; turn.

Rep last 2 rows 4 times more—12 (14, 16) sts.

Size 6 only—Next Row: Ch 2, hdc in first st, hdc2tog over next 2 sts, work Pat to end of row; turn—15 sts.

All Sizes: Cont even in Stripe Pat until armhole measures approx 5 (6, 6)", ending with WS row. Fasten off.

BACK

With RS facing, sk next 6 (4, 4) sts; join appropriate color to next st; ch 2— counts as hdc; work Pat across next 45 (49, 53) sts; turn, leaving rem sts unworked. Cont even in Stripe Pat on 46 (50, 54) sts until armhole measures approx 5 (6, 6)", ending with a WS row. Fasten off.

LEFT FRONT

With RS facing, sk 6 (4, 4) sts; join appropriate color to next st, ch 2; work Pat to end of row—22 (24, 26) sts; turn. Work to correspond to Right Front, reversing all shapings.

SLEEVE (make 2)

Beg at lower edge with A, ch 28 (30, 30).

Row 1 (RS): Hdc in 3rd ch from hook, hdc in each ch across; turn—26 (28, 28) sts.

Rows 2–4: Cont in Stripe Pat as est.

Row 5 (RS): Ch 2—counts as hdc; 2 hdc in first st, work Pat to last st, 2 hdc in last st; turn.

Row 6: Work even in pat.

Rep last 2 rows 3 (7, 4) times more—34 (44, 38) sts.

Next Row (RS): Ch 2, 2 hdc in first st, work Pat to last st, 2 hdc in last st; turn. Work 3 rows even in Pat.

Rep last 4 rows 2 (1, 4) time(s) more—40 (48, 48) sts.

Work even in Pat to approx 9½ (11, 13½)" from beg, ending with a WS row. Place markers on each side ¾ (¾, 1)" down from last row.

finishing

Sew shoulder seams. Sew sleeve seams to markers.

Sew in Sleeves, placing rows above markers along unworked sts of Front and Back armholes to form square armholes.

BOTTOM AND NECK EDGING

Rnd 1: With RS facing, join MC with sl st at bottom right corner. Work 1 rnd of sc evenly up Right Front, around Back neck, down Left Front and around bottom edge of Body; join with sl st to first sc.

Place markers for 5 buttonholes on Right (or Left for boy) Front edge; place bottom marker ½" above bottom edge, top marker ½" below beg of neck shaping, and space rem 3 markers evenly bet.

Rnd 2: Ch 1; *sc in each sc to first buttonhole marker, ch 2, sk next 2 sts; rep from * 4 times more; sc in each sc to end of rnd; join with sl st to first sc.

Rnd 3: Ch 1, working from left to right (reverse sc), work sc in each sc around and 2 sc in each ch-2 sp; join with sl st to first st. Fasten off.

SLEEVE EDGING

With RS facing, join MC with sl st at sleeve seam. Work as for Bottom and Edging, omitting all directions for buttonholes. Sew buttons in place.

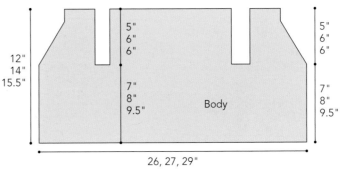

5"
6"
6"

5"
6"
6"

12"
14"
15.5"

7"
8"
9.5"

7"
8"
9.5"

Body

26, 27, 29"

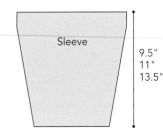

Sleeve

9.5"
11"
13.5"

diagonal duo

Crochet this afghan and pillow in a jiffy to have ready for picnics and tailgate parties. The duo makes a great send-off gift for a college student, too.

DESIGNER: STITCHWORX   PHOTOGRAPHER: PERRY STRUSE

skill level
Easy

finished measurements
Pillow = approx 16" square, excluding the border
Throw = approx 45×67"

yarns
Note: *Yarn amounts are given for the pillow. The amounts for the throw follow in parentheses.*
Lion Brand Jiffy (Art. 450); 100% acrylic; 3 oz. (85 g); 135 yds. (123 m); light bulky weight (See Note below.)
- 2 (6) balls #181 Country Green (A)
- 2 (8) balls #111 Heather Blue (B)
- 2 (4) balls #105 Pastel Blue (C)

Note: *Heather Blue yarn comes in 2½-oz. (70-g), 115-yd. (103-m) balls.*

hooks & extra
- Size Q/19 (15.75 mm) crochet hook for the pillow *or size needed to obtain gauge*
- Size K/10½ (6.5 mm) crochet hook for the throw *or size needed to obtain gauge*
- 16"-square pillow form

gauge
Pillow: In hdc with a double strand of yarn, 5 sts = 9" (12.7 cm); 5 rows = 4" (10 cm).
Throw: In hdc with a double strand of yarn, 6 sts and 16 rows = 4" (10 cm).
TAKE TIME TO CHECK YOUR GAUGE.

Notes: *When working the strips, cut and join the colors for each new strip. To change a color in half double crochet (hdc): With the current color, yarn over and draw up a loop in the last stitch; with the next color, complete the hdc. Crochet over the ends as you go.*

pillow
FRONT
First Half (triangle shape): With a double strand of C, ch 2.
Row 1 (RS): Hdc in 2nd ch from hook; turn work.
Row 2: Ch 1, 3 hdc in hdc; turn.
Row 3: Ch 1, 2 hdc in hdc, hdc in hdc, 2 hdc in hdc, changing to A in last st—5 sts; turn.
Row 4: With A, ch 1, 2 hdc in first hdc, hdc in 3 hdc, 2 hdc in last hdc—7 sts; turn work.
Row 5: With A, ch 1, 2 hdc in first hdc, hdc in 5 hdc, 2 hdc in last hdc changing to C in last st—9 sts; turn.
Rows 6–15: Cont in hdc, inc 1 st each edge every row in the following color sequence: Work 2 rows C, 2 rows B, 4 rows A, 2 rows B—29 sts. The shape should measure approx 16" across. Mark the end of this row for the bottom edge.
Second Half—Row 1: With C, ch 1, hdc in first hdc, hdc2tog, hdc in each hdc across to last 3 sts, hdc2tog, hdc in last st—27 sts; turn work.
Rows 2–12: Rep Row 1 in the following color sequence: Work 1 more row with C, 4 rows B, 4 rows A, and 2 rows B—5 sts rem.
Row 13: With B, ch 1, hdc2tog, hdc in hdc, hdc2tog; turn.
Row 14: With B, ch 1, hdc3tog. Fasten off.

BACK
Work as for the Front, but the even-numbered rows are RS rows.

pillow
Holding WS tog so that the stripes match, attach C in any corner with a sl st and through both sides.
Working through both layers to join, ch 1, (3 hdc in corner, 14 hdc evenly spaced along side edge) 3 times, 3 hdc in corner. Insert pillow form.
Work 14 hdc evenly across the last edge to close the opening. Join with a sl st in first hdc.
Ch 1, hdc in same hdc as joining; working 3 hdc in each corner, hdc in each hdc around. Join and fasten off.
With RS facing, join A with a sl st in any hdc. Working left to right for rev sc, make 1 rev sc in each hdc around. At end, join. Fasten off.

throw
FIRST SECTION
(bottom triangle—horizontal shaping)
With a double strand of A, ch 2.
Row 1 (RS): Hdc in 2nd ch from hook; turn work.
Row 2: Ch 1, 3 hdc in hdc, changing to B in last st; turn.
Row 3: With B, ch 1, 2 hdc in first hdc, hdc in next hdc, 2 hdc in last hdc—5 sts; turn work.
Row 4: With B, ch 1, 2 hdc in first hdc, hdc in next 3 hdc, 2 hdc in last hdc—7 sts; turn.
Rows 5–38: Cont in hdc, inc 1 st each edge every row in the following color sequence: Work 4 rows more with B, 2 rows A, 2 rows C, 2 rows A, 6 rows B, 6 rows C, 2 rows A, 2 rows C, 2 rows B, 4 rows A, 2 rows B—75 sts.
Mark end of this row for bottom edge.

SECOND SECTION

(center—vertical shaping)

Row 1 (RS): Ch 1, hdc in first st, 2 hdc in next st, work to last 3 sts, hdc2tog, hdc in last st—75 sts; turn.

Row 2: Ch 1, hdc in first st, hdc2tog, work to last 2 sts, 2 hdc in next st, hdc in last st—75 sts; turn.

Rows 3–18: Rep Rows 1 and 2 in the following color sequence: Work 2 rows C, 4 rows B, 4 rows A, 4 rows B, and 2 rows C.

THIRD SECTION

(top triangle—horizontal shaping)

Row 1 (RS): With B, ch 1, hdc in first st, hdc2tog, work to last 3 sts, hdc2tog, hdc in last st—73 sts; turn.

Rows 2–36: Rep Row 1 in the following color sequence: Work 1 row more in B, 4 rows A, 2 rows B, 2 rows C, 2 rows A, 6 rows C, 6 rows B, 2 rows A, 2 rows C, 2 rows A, and 6 rows B.

Row 37: With A, hdc2tog, hdc in next hdc, hdc2tog; turn.

Row 38: With A, hdc3tog. Fasten off.

BORDER

Join B in any corner with a sl st.

Ch 1, 3 hdc in same corner as joining. Work 66 hdc evenly spaced along each long edge, 44 hdc evenly spaced along each short edge, and 3 hdc in each corner. At the end, join with a sl st in first hdc.

Ch 1, hdc in same hdc as joining; working 3 hdc in each corner, hdc in each hdc around; join and fasten off. With the RS facing, join A with a sl st in any hdc.

Working left to right for rev sc, make 1 rev sc in each hdc around. At end, join and fasten off.

crochet tips

■ When you're working a length of chains, the loop on the hook never counts as a stitch. For example, "ch 50" means to work 50 chain stitches plus the slip knot and the loop on the hook.

■ Turning chains always count as the first stitch of a new row or round, except when you single-crochet.

● A long dash (—) in a pattern is a reference point only. The information following the dash tells you how many stitches you have worked, or it names a special pattern stitch you have just completed (such as a cluster or shell). The pattern stitch will not be repeated in the directions. Refer to the information preceding the dash to repeat the pattern stitch when it's required.

■ Check knitters' tools at your yarn store. You'll find lots of gadgets there that work equally well for crocheters.

■ If you think you're going to run out of yarn in the middle of a row, attach a new ball of yarn before beginning the row.

■ When instructions don't tell you where to work a stitch, always work under the two top loops. Directions will be specific when you should work into the back or front loops. When you're joining a round with a slip stitch, always work the slip stitch under the top two loops of a stitch to avoid a clumsy hole.

fringed afghan and pillow

Variegated pastel yarn gives this afghan and pillow the gentle look of a Monet watercolor. The loop edging on the afghan and the loop-covered front on the pillow coordinate the set.

DESIGNER: ANNA MISHKA
PHOTOGRAPHER: JASON WILDE

skill level
Beginner

finished measurements
Afghan = 36×45", excluding fringe
Pillow = 14" square

yarns
Lion Brand Watercolors; 65% acrylic/35% wool; 1¾ oz. (50 g); 55 yds. (50 m); bulky weight
- 14 skeins #300 Shell for afghan
- 4 skeins #300 Shell for pillow

hooks & extras
For the afghan
- Size N/15 (10 mm) crochet hook *or size needed to obtain gauge*
- Blunt-end yarn needle

For the pillow
- Size L/11 (8 mm) crochet hook *or size needed to obtain gauge*
- 14" square pillow form
- Blunt-end yarn needle

gauge
Afghan: With larger hook in Seed st pat, 9 sts and 9 rows = 4" (10 cm).
Pillow: With smaller hook, 8 sc and 8 rows = 4" (10 cm).
TAKE TIME TO CHECK YOUR GAUGE.

special stitches
Loop Stitch (Lp st)
To make lps when working scs, insert hook into st and draw up yarn from behind the index finger to shape a 2" or 4" long lp; then draw yarn from the ball through the 2 lps on the hook to complete the sc and secure the lp.

afghan
With larger hook, ch 78.
Foundation Row (RS): Sc in 2nd ch from hook; *ch 1, sk ch, sc in next ch; rep from * across—77 sts; turn.
Row 1: Ch 1, sc in sc and ch-1 sp; *ch 1, sk next sc, sc in next ch-1 sp; rep from * across; end with sc in last sc; turn.
Row 2: Ch 1, sc in first sc; *ch 1, sk next sc, sc in ch-1 sp; rep from * across; end with ch 1, sk next sc, sc in last sc; turn.
Rep Rows 1 and 2 until piece measures approx 43" from beg, ending with a RS row; fasten off.
Loop Edging—Rnd 1: With RS facing, join yarn with sl st in top right corner, ch 1, sc in same st. Work 75 more sc evenly across top of afghan, 3 sc in corner, 96 sc down left side of afghan, 3 sc in corner, 75 sc across bottom of afghan, 3 sc in corner, 96 sc up right side of afghan, 2 sc in same st as first sc—354 sc; join with sl st in first sc.
Rnd 2: Ch 1, sc in same sc as sl st; *make a 4" Lp st in next sc; rep from * around; join with sl st in first sc; fasten off.

pillow

BACK

With smaller hook, ch 30.

Foundation Row (RS): Sc in 2nd ch from hook and in each ch across—29 sts; turn.

Row 1: Ch 1, working in front lps, sc in each sc across; turn.

Row 2: Ch 1, working in back lps, sc in each sc across; turn.

Rep Rows 1 and 2 to approx 14" from beg, ending with Row 1; fasten off.

FRONT

Row 1 (RS): Ch 1, sc in first sc; *sc a 2" Lp st in next sc; rep from * across; turn.

Row 2: Ch 1, sc in each sc across; turn.

Row 3: Ch 1, sc in first 2 sc; *Lp st in next sc, sc in next sc; rep from * across, ending Lp st in next sc, sc in next 2 sc; turn.

Row 4: Rep Row 2. Rep Rows 1–4 until piece from beg measures approx 14", ending with a WS row; fasten off.

finishing

With WS facing, whipstitch Front to Back on 3 sides; insert pillow form and sew rem side closed.

sherling suede
blanket and pillow

The allure of suede, created with nylon ribbon yarn, gives this easy pattern a rich elegance. The basic stitch for both projects is half double crochet, but it's the choice of natural colors that makes this a stand-out set.

DESIGNER: CANDI JENSEN
PHOTOGRAPHER: JASON WILDE

skill level
Beginner

finished measurements
Blanket = 50×61½"
Pillow = 16" square

yarns
Berroco Suede; 100% nylon; 1¾ oz. (50 g); 120 yds. (110 m); worsted weight
- 20 balls #3714 Hopalong Cassidy for blanket
- 2 balls #3714 Hopalong Cassidy for pillow

Berroco Plush; 100% nylon; 1¾ oz. (50 g); 90 yds. (82 m); worsted weight
- 3 balls #1901 Crema for blanket
- 2 balls #1901 Crema for pillow

hook & extras
- Size H/8 (5 mm) crochet hook *or size needed to obtain gauge*
- Blunt-end yarn needle
- 16"-square pillow form

gauge
With Suede, 14 hdc and 12 rows = 4" (10 cm).
Rectangle measures approx 15½×19½".
With Plush, 11 hdc and 8 rows = 4" (10 cm).
TAKE TIME TO CHECK YOUR GAUGE.

blanket
RECTANGLE (make 9)
With Suede, ch 55.
Foundation Row (RS): Hdc in 2nd ch from hook and in each ch across—54 sts; turn.
Row 1: Ch 1, hdc in each hdc across; turn.
Rows 2–58: Rep Row 1. Fasten off.
Edging: With RS facing, join Plush with a sl st in corner at beg of last row; in same st work ch 1, sc, ch 2, and sc. Adjusting st placement as necessary, (ch 1, sk next st, sc in next st) 26 times; in corner work ch 1, sc, ch 2 and sc; working along next side, work (ch 1, sk next row, sc in side of next row) 28 times; in corner work ch 1, sc, ch 2, and sc; working along next side, work (ch 1, sk next st, sc in next st) 26 times; in corner work ch 1, sc, ch 2, and sc; working along next side, work (ch 1, sk next row, sc in side of next row) 28 times, ch 1; join with sl st to first sc. Fasten off.

finishing
With RS facing, assemble the blanket by whipstitching the Rectangles tog into 3 strips wide by 3 strips long.
Border—Rnd 1: With WS facing, join Plush in any ch-1 sp, ch 2—counts as hdc; hdc in same sp; 2 hdc in each ch-1 sp around, working 2 hdc, ch 2, and 2 hdc in each corner ch-2 sp; join with sl st in 2nd ch of beg ch-2; turn.
Rnd 2: Ch 1, sc in same st as join; sc in each hdc and ch-2 sp around, adjusting

sts by increasing or decreasing to keep edges flat; join with sl st in first sc. Fasten off.

pillow

FRONT SQUARE (make 4)
With Suede, ch 32. Hdc in 2nd ch from hook and in each ch across—31 sts; turn.
Row 1: Ch 1, hdc in each hdc across; turn.
Rows 2–20: Rep Row 1. Fasten off.

Edging: With RS facing, join Plush with sl st in top right hdc; in same st work ch 1 and sc. Adjusting st placement to come out evenly, (ch 1, sk 1 st, sc in next st) 13 times; working along side, ch 1, sc in first row, (ch 1, sk row, sc in next row) 10 times. Fasten off.

BACK
With Plush, ch 46. Hdc in 2nd ch from hook and in each ch across—45 sts; turn.

Row 1: Ch 1, hdc in each hdc across; turn. Rep Row 1 until piece measures approx 17" from beg. Fasten off.

finishing

Matching edgings, whipstitch Front Squares tog with Plush. With RS tog and Plush, sew 3 sides of pillow Front and Back tog; turn RS out. Insert pillow form; sew last side closed.

homespun
welcome mat

Set this shell-pattern rug at your entryway to make a welcoming and impressive statement.
For safety's sake, be sure to place a nonslip pad under the rug on a smooth surface.

DESIGNER: CATHERINE ENG
PHOTOGRAPHER: PERRY STRUSE

skill level
Easy

finished measurements
27×37", excluding fringe

yarns
Lion Brand Homespun (Art. 790); 98% acrylic/2% polyester; 6 oz. (170 g); 185 yds. (167 m); bulky weight
● 2 skeins #344 Arcadian* (A)
● 4 skeins #347 Mediterranean (B)

As we went to press, #344 Arcadian had been discontinued; substitute a similar color.

hook
● Size N/13 (9 mm) crochet hook *or size needed to obtain gauge*

gauge
(1 sc, 1 lg shell, 1 sc) = 3".
Row 1 = 1¼" high.
TAKE TIME TO CHECK YOUR GAUGE.

pattern stitches
Large Shell = 5 dc; **Small Shell** = 3 dc

Notes: Rug is worked with two strands held together throughout. Foundation chain is the lengthwise center of the rug. Leave 5" tails when beginning and fastening off to tie into final fringe. To begin a new color, draw up a loop in the end stitch. Chain-3 counts as one double crochet.

instructions
First Side
Foundation Ch: With B, ch 86.
Row 1 (RS): Sc in 2nd ch from hook. *Sk 2 ch, 5 dc in next ch—Large Shell made, sk 2 ch, sc in next ch; rep from * across—14 shells. Fasten off. With A, draw up lp in end sc.
Row 2 (WS): Ch 3, turn, dc in same sc. *Ch 1, sc in center dc of next shell, ch 1, 3 dc in next sc—Small Shell made; rep from * across, end with ch 1, 2 dc in last dc. Fasten off. With B, draw up a lp in end dc.
Row 3 (RS): Ch 1, sc in same dc. *5 dc in next sc, sc in center dc of next shell; rep from * across, end sc in top of ch-3.
Row 4: With B, rep Row 2.
Row 5: With B, rep Row 3.
Row 6: With A, rep Row 2. Fasten off.
Row 7: With B, rep Row 3. Fasten off.
Row 8: With A, rep Row 2. Fasten off.
Rows 9–11: With B, rep Rows 3, 2, and 3, using B for Rows 9 and 11 and A for Row 10. Fasten off after Row 11.
Row 12: With A, rep Row 2. Fasten off.
Rows 13–15: Rep Rows 3, 2, and 3, using B for Rows 13 and 15 and A for Row 14. Fasten off after Row 15.
Row 16: With A, rep Row 2.
Row 17: Ch 1, turn. Sc in first dc, ch 2, sc in next sc, *ch 2, (sc, ch 2, sc) in center dc of next shell, ch 2, sc in next sc; rep from * across, end ch 2, sc in last dc. Fasten off.

Second Side
Draw up a lp in end ch on opposite side of Foundation Ch. Ch 1, sc in same ch. Rep rem of Row 1, then Rows 2–17.

finishing
Cut 10" yarn lengths to match the colors at the ends of rows for fringe. Pull 2 lengths through the end of each row with tails and 3 lengths through the end of each row without tails (each end of dc row needs 2 fringes; pull length through top and over post of dc). Tie in an overhand knot. Trim to 4".

happy daisy
pillow

Bring sunshine into a little one's day with this cheerful accent pillow. Use traditional daisy colors or choose yarns that match the child's room.

DESIGNER: ANNA MISHKA
PHOTOGRAPHERS: MARTY BALDWIN (OPPOSITE BOTTOM), ANDY LYONS (OPPOSITE TOP)

skill level
Beginner

finished measurements
Pillow = approx 33" in diameter, including petals

yarns
Lion Brand Wool-Ease; 80% acrylic/ 20% wool; 3 oz. (85 g); 197 yds. (177 m); worsted weight
• 2 balls #158 Buttercup (MC)
• Small amount #153 Black (B)

Lion Brand Polarspun; 100% polyester; 1¾ oz. (50 g); 137 yds. (123 m); bulky weight
• 4 balls #100 Snow White (A)

hooks & extras
• Size H/8 (5 mm) crochet hook *or size needed to obtain gauge*
• Size J/10 (6 mm) crochet hook *or size needed to obtain gauge*
• 1 lb. polyester stuffing
• Blunt-end yarn needle

gauge
With smaller hook and MC, 15 sc and 16 rows = 4" (10 cm).
With larger hook and A, 12 sts and 12 rows = 4"(10 cm).
TAKE TIME TO CHECK YOUR GAUGE.

instructions
DAISY CENTER BASE (make 2)
Beg at lower edge with smaller hook and MC, ch 10.
Row 1 (WS): Sc in 2nd ch from hook and in each ch across—9 sc; turn.
Row 2: Ch 4, sc in 2nd ch from hook and in next 2 ch, sc in each sc across; end with 2 sc in last sc—13 sc; turn.
Row 3: Rep Row 2—17 sc; turn.
Row 4: Ch 3, sc in 2nd ch from hook and in next ch, sc in each sc across; end with 2 sc in last sc—20 sc; turn.
Row 5: Rep Row 4—23 sc; turn.
Row 6: Ch 1, 2 sc in first sc, sc in each sc across; end with 2 sc in last sc—25 sc; turn.
Rows 7–9: Rep Row 6. At end of Row 9—31 sc.
Row 10: Ch 1, sc in each sc across; turn.
Rows 11–25: Cont in sc, inc 1 st each edge on Rows 11, 13, 14, 16, 18, 22, and 25. At end of Row 25, there are 45 sts. Cont in sc on 45 sts for 14 more rows. Beg to dec as foll:
Row 1 (RS): Ch 1, sk first sc, sc in each sc across, end with sk next sc, sc in last sc—43 sts; turn.
Rows 2 and 3: Work even.
Row 4: Rep Row 1—41 sc.
Rows 5–20: Cont in sc pat and dec 1 st each edge on Rows 8, 10, 12, 13, 15, 17, 18, 19, and 20. At end of Row 20—23 sts.
Row 21: Ch 1, sk first sc, sc in each sc across, leaving last 2 sts unworked—20 sts; turn.
Row 22: Rep Row 21—17 sts.

Row 23: Ch 1, sk first sc, sc in each sc across, leaving last 3 sts unworked—13 sts; turn.
Row 24: Rep Row 23—9 sts; fasten off.

DAISY PETAL (make 10)
With larger hook and A, ch 32.
Foundation Row (RS): Sc in 2nd ch from hook; *ch 1, sk ch, sc in next ch; rep from * across—31 sts; turn.
Row 1 (WS): Ch 1, sc in first sc; *sc in ch-1 sp, ch 1, sk sc; rep from * across; end with sc in ch-1 sp, sc in sc; turn.
Row 2: Ch 1, sc in first sc; *ch 1, sk sc, sc in next ch-1 sp; rep from * across; end with ch 1, sk sc, sc in last sc; turn.
Rep Rows 1 and 2 until work from beg measures approx 7", ending with Row 1.
Shape top: Ch 1, work in pat across, leaving last 3 sts unworked—28 sts; turn. Rep last row until 7 sts rem; fasten off.

finishing
Run a contrasting line of basting down the vertical center on the front of one base; rep for the horizontal center. With WS tog, sew the 2 base pieces tog, leaving an opening; stuff firmly. Sew opening closed. With RS tog, sew petals tog in pairs, leaving straight edges open; turn RS out and stuff lightly. Sew first petal onto top of base, centered over the vertical basting line. Pin rem 4 petals around base to resemble arms and legs, easing to fit; sew in place.

FEATURES
Hold the pillow base so the longest portion is vertical.
Eyes: Place stitch markers 6 sts above the basting center and 5 sts to each side. For each eye, embroider 4 color B straight sts over 5 rows and 4 more color B straight sts toward the outside edge over 5 rows.
Mouth: Place a marker 17 rows below the center; count 10 rows to each side and go up 8 rows; place markers for beg and end of embroidery. Work a stem st smile bet markers. Remove basting.

Better Homes and Gardens®
Creative Collection™

Editorial Director
Gayle Goodson Butler

Editor-in-Chief
Beverly Rivers

Executive Editor Karman Wittry Hotchkiss

Contributing Editorial Manager Heidi Palkovic

Contributing Design Director Tracy DeVenney

Contributing Project Editor Laura Holtorf Collins
Copy Chief Mary Heaton
Contributing Copy Editor Pegi Bevins
Contributing Proofreader Joleen Ross
Administrative Assistant Lori Eggers

Executive Vice President
Bob Mate

Publishing Group President
Jack Griffin

Chairman and CEO William T. Kerr
President and COO Stephen M. Lacy

In Memoriam
E. T. Meredith III (1933–2003)